HAMLYN ALL COLOUR BOOK OF
Cakes and Cake Decorating

HAMLYN ALL COLOUR BOOK OF
Cakes and Cake Decorating
Jill Spencer

Hamlyn
London·New York·Sydney·Toronto

CONTENTS

Useful facts and figures	10
Introduction	12
Cake making equipment	14
Cake making methods	16
Icing equipment	18
Traditional favourites	20
Small cakes and biscuits	46
Special occasion cakes	66
Gâteaux	82
Novelty cakes	100
Icings and decorations	112
Index	124

Photography by Fred Mancini
Illustrations by Christina Mingard
The publishers would like to thank Baker Smith Cake Decorations Limited and T.I.
Tower Housewares Limited for providing products for use in the photographs.
Published by The Hamlyn Publishing Group Limited
London · New York · Sydney · Toronto
Astronaut House, Feltham, Middlesex, England
ISBN 0 600 32225 4
Fourth impression 1982

Useful facts and figures

Notes on metrication
In this book quantities are given in metric and Imperial measures. Exact conversion from Imperial to metric measure does not usually give very convenient working quantities and so the metric measures have been rounded off into units of 25 grams. The table below shows the recommended equivalents.

Ounces	Approx g to nearest whole figure	Recommended conversion to nearest unit of 25
1	28	25
2	57	50
3	85	75
4	113	100
5	142	150
6	170	175
7	198	200
8	227	225
9	255	250
10	283	275
11	312	300
12	340	350
13	368	375
14	396	400
15	425	425
16 (1 lb)	454	450

Note: When converting quantities over 20 oz first add the appropriate figures in the centre column, then adjust to the nearest unit of 25. As a general guide, 1 kg (1000 g) equals 2.2 lb or about 2 lb 3 oz. This method of conversion gives good results in nearly all cases, although in certain pastry and cake recipes a more accurate conversion is necessary to produce a balanced recipe.

Liquid measures The millilitre has been used in this book and the following table gives a few examples.

Imperial	Approx ml to nearest whole figure	Recommended ml
¼ pint	142	150 ml
½ pint	283	300 ml
¾ pint	425	450 ml
1 pint	567	600 ml
1½ pints	851	900 ml
1¾ pints	992	1000 ml (1 litre)

Spoon measures All spoon measures given in this book are level unless otherwise stated.

Can sizes At present, cans are marked with the exact (usually to the nearest whole number) metric equivalent of the Imperial weight of the contents, so we have followed this practice when giving can sizes.

Note: When making any of the recipes in this book, only follow one set of measures as they are not interchangeable.

10

Oven temperatures

	°C	°F	Gas Mark
Very cool	110	225	¼
	120	250	½
Cool	140	275	1
	150	300	2
Moderate	160	325	3
	180	350	4
Moderately hot	190	375	5
	200	400	6
Hot	220	425	7
	230	450	8
Very hot	240	475	9

Notes for American and Australian users
In America the 8-oz measuring cup is used. In Australia metric measures are now used in conjunction with the standard 250-ml measuring cup. The Imperial pint, used in Britain and Australia, is 20 fl oz, while the American pint is 16 fl oz. It is important to remember that the Australian tablespoon differs from both the British and American tablespoons; the table below gives a comparison. The British standard tablespoon, which has been used throughout this book, holds 17.7 ml, the American 14.2 ml, and the Australian 20 ml. A teaspoon holds approximately 5 ml in all three countries.

British	American	Australian
1 teaspoon	1 teaspoon	1 teaspoon
1 tablespoon	1 tablespoon	1 tablespoon
2 tablespoons	3 tablespoons	2 tablespoons
3½ tablespoons	4 tablespoons	3 tablespoons
4 tablespoons	5 tablespoons	3½ tablespoons

An Imperial/American guide to solid and liquid measures

Solid measures

IMPERIAL	AMERICAN
1 lb butter or margarine	2 cups
1 lb flour	4 cups
1 lb granulated or castor sugar	2 cups
1 lb icing sugar	3 cups
8 oz rice	1 cup

Liquid measures

IMPERIAL	AMERICAN
¼ pint liquid	⅔ cup liquid
½ pint	1¼ cups
¾ pint	2 cups
1 pint	2½ cups
1½ pints	3¾ cups
2 pints	5 cups (2½ pints)

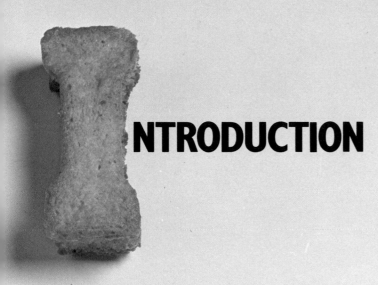

INTRODUCTION

There is nothing quite so appetising and tempting as the aroma of a cake being baked and more and more people are becoming interested in this particular aspect of cookery. It is very rewarding to be able to produce home baked cakes, gâteaux and special occasion cakes for your family and guests.

This book has been written to cover the widest possible range and there is also a chapter devoted to icings and decorations, with step by step illustrations. All the traditional favourites are included as well as some ideas that might be new to you. Whether you are an experienced cook or just a beginner, there is something for everyone from a simply iced basic Victoria sandwich to a sophisticated wedding cake.

For those eager to be a little adventurous there are some exciting and original ideas for children's novelty cakes.

Presentation, whether it be a simple iced cake or a more elaborately decorated gâteau is all important, and it isn't difficult with this book as your guide to achieve a professional finish. We have included some simple yet effective ways of icing as well as the more advanced techniques of royal icing.

Cake decorations are fun to make although they require a little more patience. These have been illustrated with step by step photographs showing the various stages making it easy for you to follow.

With the aid of today's appliances, such as food mixers and processors and freezers, baking is much easier for even the busiest housewives. Mixers take the hard work out of creaming and whisking making it worthwhile to do batch baking for the freezer. Cakes and biscuits are particularly good freezer candidates, so you can always have a selection to offer to unexpected guests.

I would like to thank Bridget Jones for her help in writing this book and in particular for her patience in creating the delightful novelty cakes. I hope you will gain as much pleasure from using the recipes as I have had in creating them and preparing the cakes for photography.

Cake making equipment

There is a vast selection of tins available on the market, varying in shape, size and type of finish. The price range is as broad as the choice and is usually significant of the quality. It is not necessary to own a wide variety of tins; a small selection of basic tins is quite adequate for most baking purposes. This should include a pair of sandwich tins, a deep cake tin, a loaf tin and a Swiss roll tin. The type of finish chosen when buying tins should be considered in terms of the price, the quality desired and the expected usage of the tins. For instance, tins that are likely to be used frequently need to be of better quality than a tin which may only be used on certain occasions. It is worth remembering that good quality tins, well looked after, will last a long time.

There are many types of non-stick finishes and coatings available, some of which are very effective. However, some of the inexpensive non-stick tins may be disappointing if they are to receive heavy use. There are many different shapes of tins including round deep cake tins, sandwich tins, square and oblong cake tins, loaf tins, Swiss roll tins and some unusual decorative tins. Loose-bottomed tins, both round and square, are useful when baking large or delicate cakes. Spring form tins are round tins which have loose bottoms and sides. The side has a clip attached to a spring which, when released, frees the base from its groove. Adjustable loaf tins are slightly unusual. Each section of these tins is clipped together and may be extended to give a larger tin. Removal of cakes from these tins is easy due to the fact that the sides drop away leaving the cake on the base.

It is most important that cake tins are well treated, to ensure that they are effective and have a long life. The manufacturer's instructions for use, cleaning and storage should always be strictly followed, however there are a few general points to remember. Most tins should be well greased before using and should be washed or soaked immediately after use. Abrasive cleaning powders and pads should be avoided. Sharp or pointed knives should never be used to remove cakes from their tins or to cut anything in the tin. Metal objects should generally not be used with non-stick tins except with extreme care. Tins should be stored in a dry, ventilated cupboard where they will not rust. Non-stick tins should not be stacked together without some form of wrapping or interleaving to prevent scratching.

A recipe may call for the tin to be lined or coated with flour. A lightly greased tin may be coated with flour by sprinkling a little flour into it and tapping gently whilst tilting the tin to spread the flour evenly. Any excess flour should be tipped out. Other linings include greaseproof paper, non-stick parchment and rice paper. The lining used should fit the tin smoothly and exactly. If the tin is to be bottomed-lined, the outline of the base should be drawn on the paper, cut out and placed in the tin.

To line a straight sided round or square tin Draw around the base of the tin on greaseproof paper and cut out a circle slightly smaller than the tin. Cut a strip of greaseproof paper long enough to go around the inside of the tin and approximately 5 cm/2 inches deeper than the tin. Make a 2.5-cm/1-inch fold along the length of the strip and snip it all along at intervals of approximately 1 cm/½ inch. The greaseproof paper will adhere to the sides of the tin if they are lightly greased. Place the strip around the inside of the tin, overlapping the slits in the base. Grease the sides well then place the circle of greaseproof paper in the base and grease well. The paper should sit slightly above the side of the tin.

To line a Swiss roll or loaf tin Place the tin on a sheet of greaseproof paper allowing enough paper on each side to come up the sides of the tin and overlap slightly at the top. Draw around the shape of the tin and cut out an oblong of paper allowing for the depth of the sides. Cut inwards from each corner to the corner point on the outline of the tin. Lower the paper into the base of the lightly greased tin with the bottom of each slit in the base of each corner. Neatly fold and overlap the cut greaseproof paper inside each corner, greasing the piece lying underneath slightly in order to hold both pieces flat. Grease the paper well before placing the mixture in the tin.

All the tins in this book have been identified in terms of their dimensions apart from loaf tins. In this case we have used either a 450-g/1-lb or 1-kg/2-lb tin.

15

Cake making methods

The basic ingredients that go into making a cake are fat, flour, sugar and eggs. The texture of the cake is governed by the method of preparation and the proportions of ingredients.

The methods of cake making have been revolutionised over the years although we still have some of the traditional methods. With the introduction of the soft margarines, came the all-in-one method of cake-making. All the ingredients are put into a bowl and beaten together until smooth. As there is no creaming involved to incorporate air, which in turn makes the cake rise, extra raising agent is required when using this method.

The creaming method is probably the most well known and widely used method. The fat and sugar are beaten together until pale and fluffy in texture, before the other ingredients are added.

The rubbing-in method is used, for making less rich cakes and some biscuit mixtures.

The melting method is very easy and used in the making of gingerbreads, brandy snaps etc. The fat, syrup and sugar are melted over a low heat, before adding the other ingredients.

The whisking method is used for fatless sponges,

16

Swiss rolls and genoese-type cakes. The sugar and eggs are whisked in a basin over hot water until really thick and creamy.

Helpful hints

Positions of cakes in the oven Unless otherwise stated, cakes should always be cooked in the centre of the oven. If there is not a true centre shelf, then use a slightly lower rather than a higher shelf. If you are cooking two cakes at once, place them underneath each other rather than on the same shelf, and change positions half way through cooking.

Temperature of ingredients All ingredients should be at room temperature before use to ensure a successful cake.

Ovens Always preheat the oven for at least 15 minutes before using. Individual ovens vary in temperature, so it is important to know your oven, especially where cakes are concerned.

Measuring spoons All spoon measurements refer to the British Standard measuring spoons, which are plastic and can be purchased in any good department store.

Fruit Dried fruit is normally purchased ready for use, but if it is not, wash and rub dry in a teatowel. Leave in a warm place until completely dry.

Eggs The EEC regulations now stipulate that eggs must be graded according to their weight and numbered accordingly. We have used a size 3 egg throughout all the recipes unless otherwise stipulated. It is important to use the correct size of egg particularly when using the metric measurements, as cake recipes are particularly critical.

Testing a cake The most reliable way of testing a cake to see if it is cooked is to insert a metal skewer into the middle of the cake. If it comes out clean, the cake is ready. Another method is to gently press the centre of the cake. If it is firm and beginning to shrink away from the sides of the tin, then it is cooked.

Freezing All cakes and biscuits freeze well. Cakes can be frozen either iced or un-iced depending upon the type of icing. Butter and fudge icing freeze well, but glacé icing, frosting and royal icing are not to be recommended. It is not necessary to freeze rich fruit cakes as they improve with keeping for up to 6 months.

If freezing a layered type cake, wrap each layer with a sheet of greaseproof paper and pack in a polythene bag or rigid container.

If freezing an iced cake, open freeze on a baking sheet until really firm, then pack in a rigid container. Gâteaux and novelty cakes are particularly suitable for this method of freezing, but it is advisable to put the final decorations on when the cake has thawed.

Icing equipment

The phrase, the right tool for the right job, is very relevant when applied to the art of icing. Using the correct piece of equipment not only makes icing easy but also fun! There is a fantastic range of equipment on the market to choose from, but to begin with, one only needs the basics.

Piping bags These can be purchased or hand-made. The purchased bags are usually nylon or plastic and are generally fairly large. Basically, they are designed to accommodate the larger nozzles, although some have a special screw attachment which permits the use of small nozzles. Hand-made greaseproof paper bags are suitable for royal icing as they are more controllable for fine work (see page 118 for making hand-made bag instructions.)

Piping nozzles These are made in both metal and plastic. The metal ones are generally better as they give more definition. Always buy good quality nozzles, checking that the tip of the nozzle is a perfect shape and free from any dents. The seam where the metal has been joined should be smooth to the touch. The larger nozzles are suitable for piping butter icings, meringues, choux pastry, cream etc. Whereas the small nozzles are used for piping more intricate work on wedding cakes etc. Some tubes have a thread enabling them to be used in conjunction with the screw attachments.

Cake boards These can be bought in a variety of sizes and thicknesses and come in either silver or gold. Ideal for large celebration and novelty cakes.

Turntables These are by no means essential but an absolute boon to those who do a lot of royal iced cakes. If you don't want to go to the expense of purchasing a turntable, place the board containing the cake on a upturned plate. To make it a little easier to pipe around the bottom edge, stand the plate on a large upturned bowl, ensuring it is stable.

Straight edge This is a smooth metal rule without any markings used to flat ice cakes.

Plastic scrapers These are used to smooth the sides of cakes. They can be bought either plain or with a serrated edge.

Palette knife This is an invaluable flat bladed, pliable knife used for applying icing and making attractive designs.

Greaseproof, waxed and parchment paper These are used for runouts, lining tins, piping bags, and chocolate shapes.

Cake decorations The range of decorations available is very extensive. They can normally be purchased from large department stores or specialist shops. Decorations are normally bought for a special occasion, but it is advisable to keep some basic food colourings in the store cupboard.

Chapter

TRADITIONAL FAVOURITES

Here you will find a selection of well known traditional recipes such as Dundee cake and Battenburg together with some less usual ones. Many of these are good freezer candidates, enabling you to bake them at your leisure and always have a goody to offer unexpected guests. The rich fruit cake chart will be invaluable for making those special occasion cakes in a range of sizes.

Basic Victoria sandwich

125 g/4 oz butter or margarine
125 g/4 oz castor sugar
2 eggs
125 g/4 oz self-raising flour
Filling and decoration
3–4 tablespoons raspberry jam
icing sugar

Cream the butter and sugar together until light and fluffy. Beat in the eggs one at a time, adding a little of the flour with the second egg. Fold in the remaining flour using a metal spoon. Place the mixture in a bottom-lined and greased 20-cm/8-inch sandwich tin or in two 18-cm/7-inch sandwich tins. Bake in a moderate oven (160°C, 325°F, Gas Mark 3), 35–40 minutes for the 20-cm/8-inch cake and 25–35 minutes for the 18-cm/7-inch cakes. Turn out and cool on a wire tray.

To assemble the cake Split the larger cake and sandwich the cakes or two halves with the raspberry jam. Lay a doily on top of the cake and sprinkle with icing sugar. Carefully lift off the doily to leave a design on the surface of the cake.

Variations
All-in-one Victoria sandwich Add 1 teaspoon of baking powder to the basic recipe (above). Place *all* the ingredients in a mixing bowl and beat with a wooden spoon until well mixed (2–5 minutes). Bake as above.

Battenburg

175 g/6 oz butter or margarine
175 g/6 oz castor sugar
3 eggs
175 g/6 oz self-raising flour
1 tablespoon cocoa powder
1 tablespoon hot water
grated rind of 1 lemon
Decoration
lemon curd
450 g/1 lb almond paste (see page 116)
castor sugar

Make the cake as for the basic Victoria sandwich (see page 20). Divide the mixture in half. To one half add the cocoa powder blended in hot water and to the other add the lemon rind. Line and grease an 18-cm/7-inch square cake tin and divide the centre with a strip of folded greaseproof paper. Place the chocolate mixture in one side and the lemon in the other. Bake at (160°C, 325°F, Gas Mark 3) for 40–50 minutes.

To finish the cake Trim the edges of the cake and cut each half in two, lengthways, making four strips. Join alternate colours together in two layers, sandwiching with lemon curd. Roll the almond paste into an oblong 20 × 37-cm/8 × 15-inches. Spread the outside of the assembled cake with lemon curd and place in the centre of the almond paste. Carefully ease the almond paste around the cake with the join underneath. Trim and finish as shown in the picture.

Chequered chocolate cake

175 g/6 oz butter or margarine
175 g/6 oz castor sugar
3 eggs
175 g/6 oz self-raising flour
1½ teaspoons baking powder
2 tablespoons cocoa powder
2 tablespoons hot water
Filling
3 tablespoons apricot jam, sieved
Icing and decoration
350 g/12 oz coffee butter icing (see page 112)
toasted hazelnuts, chopped

Place all the ingredients except the cocoa powder and water in a mixing bowl and beat with a wooden spoon until well mixed. Divide the mixture in half. Blend the cocoa powder with the hot water and stir into one half of the cake mixture. Place each mixture in two bottom-lined and greased 18-cm/7-inch sandwich tins. Bake in a moderate oven (160°C, 325°F, Gas Mark 3) for 45–55 minutes. Turn out and cool on a wire tray.
To assemble the cake Using a 10-cm/4-inch and a 6-cm/2½-inch plain cutter placed inside it, cut out a ring from each cake approximately 4 cm/1½ inches wide. Reassemble the cakes, putting the chocolate ring in the plain cake and the plain ring in the chocolate cake, to give a chequered effect. Sandwich the cakes together with apricot jam.
To ice and decorate the cake Make the coffee butter icing, spread some around the sides of the cake and roll in the chopped hazelnuts. Cover the top of the cake with icing and pipe around the edges. Sprinkle with chopped hazelnuts.

Hazelnut coffee cake

100 g/4 oz butter or margarine
175 g/6 oz soft brown sugar
2 eggs
6 tablespoons milk
1 tablespoon coffee essence
75 g/3 oz hazelnuts
75 g/3 oz raisins
225 g/8 oz self-raising flour
1 teaspoon baking powder
Icing and decoration
225 g/8 oz coffee butter icing (see page 112)
toasted hazelnuts

Place all the ingredients in a mixing bowl and beat with a wooden spoon until well-mixed. Place in two bottom-lined and greased 20-cm/8-inch sandwich tins. Bake in a moderate oven (160°C, 325°F, Gas Mark 3) for 30–40 minutes. Turn out and cool on a wire tray.
To ice and decorate the cake Make the icing. Sandwich the cakes together with a little of the icing. Spread the remainder over the top of the cake, piping a border around the edge. Decorate with whole toasted hazelnuts.

Variation
To make a *Walnut coffee cake*, substitute walnuts for the hazelnuts.

Walnut cake

125 g/4 oz butter or margarine
125 g/4 oz castor sugar
2 eggs
75 g/3 oz self-raising flour
100 g/4 oz walnuts, finely chopped
1 tablespoon milk
Filling and topping
American frosting (see page 115)
halved walnuts

Cream the butter and sugar together until light and fluffy. Beat in the eggs one at a time, adding a little of the flour with the second. Fold in the remaining flour, chopped walnuts and milk. Divide the mixture between two bottom-lined and greased 18-cm/7-inch sandwich tins. Bake in a moderate oven (160°C, 325°F, Gas Mark 3) for 30–35 minutes. Turn out and cool on a wire tray.

To fill and decorate the cake Make the American frosting and use a little to sandwich the cakes together. Pour the remainder over the cake, swirling with a palette knife in decorative patterns. Sprinkle with a few walnut halves.

Coffee and pear cake

175 g/6 oz butter or margarine
175 g/6 oz soft brown sugar
3 eggs
200 g/7 oz self-raising flour
2 tablespoons coffee essence
Icing
350 g/12 oz coffee butter icing (see page 112)
1 (411-g/14½-oz) can pear halves
chopped walnuts
angelica leaves

Cream the butter and sugar together until light and fluffy. Beat in the eggs one at a time, adding a little flour with each egg after the first. Fold in the remaining flour and the coffee. Divide the mixture between two bottom-lined and greased 18-cm/7-inch sandwich tins. Bake in a moderate oven (160°C, 325°F, Gas Mark 3) for 30–40 minutes. Turn out and cool on a wire tray.

To decorate the cake Make the coffee butter icing and mix a little with two of the drained and chopped pears. Use to sandwich the cakes together. Spread some of the remaining icing around the sides, then roll in the chopped walnuts. Spread the remainder over the top of the cake and pipe a decoration around the edges. Slice the remaining pears across very thinly, keeping the pear in shape. Decorate the top with the pear halves, allowing each one to fan out slightly, and angelica leaves.

HELPFUL HINT
When folding ingredients into a creamed mixture, use a metal tablespoon and work quickly and lightly cutting into and across the mixture to retain as much air as possible.

HELPFUL HINT
To cut the pears, place them flat side down and with a sharp knife, make slices across while holding the pear in shape with the other hand.

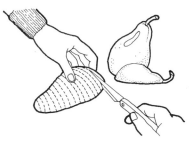

Fluted lemon caraway cake

175 g/6 oz butter or margarine
100 g/4 oz castor sugar
4 eggs
225 g/8 oz self-raising flour
1 teaspoon caraway seeds
grated rind of 1 lemon
3 tablespoons lemon curd
Icing and decoration
225 g/8 oz glacé icing (see page 114)
glacé cherries
angelica leaves

Cream the butter and sugar together until light and fluffy. Beat in the eggs one at a time, adding a little flour with each egg after the first. Fold in the remaining ingredients. Place in a greased and floured 19-cm/7½-inch fluted mould. Bake in a moderate oven (160°C, 325°F, Gas Mark 3) for 1–1¼ hours. Turn out and cool on a wire tray.
To ice and decorate the cake Make the glacé icing and pour over the cake, allowing it to run down the sides. Decorate with whole glacé cherries and angelica leaves.

Lemon curd cake

175 g/6 oz butter or margarine
175 g/6 oz castor sugar
3 eggs
175 g/6 oz self-raising flour
grated rind of 1 lemon
2 tablespoons lemon juice
Icing and decoration
225 g/8 oz lemon butter icing (see page 112)
4 tablespoons lemon curd
shredded lemon rind

Cream the butter and sugar together until light and fluffy. Add the eggs one at a time, adding a little of the flour with each egg after the first. Fold in the remaining flour with the lemon rind and juice. Place in two bottom-lined and greased 20-cm/8-inch cake tins. Bake in a moderate oven (160°C, 325°F, Gas Mark 3) for 25–35 minutes. Turn out and cool on a wire tray.
To ice and decorate the cake Make the butter icing and use a little to sandwich the cakes together. Spread the remainder over the top of the cake and using a greaseproof piping bag fitted with a star shaped nozzle, pipe a border of icing around the top edge. Heat the lemon curd very gently until runny and pour over the top of the cake, smoothing it out evenly to the edge of the piped border. Sprinkle with shredded lemon rind.

HELPFUL HINT
Rinse the angelica in hot water to soften it and to remove the sugar. This will make it a better colour and easier to cut.

Devil's food cake

175 g/6 oz butter or margarine
175 g/6 oz soft brown sugar
2 eggs
175 g/6 oz golden syrup
50 g/2 oz ground almonds
175 g/6 oz plain flour
50 g/2 oz cocoa powder
150 ml/6 fl oz milk
¼ teaspoon bicarbonate of soda
Icing and decoration
American frosting (see page 115)
chocolate curls (see page 120)

Cream the butter and sugar together until light and fluffy. Add the remaining ingredients, beating well with a wooden spoon. Pour into a lined and greased 20-cm/8-inch cake tin. Bake in a cool oven (150°C, 300°F, Gas Mark 2) for 1¾–2 hours. Turn out and cool on a wire tray.
To ice and decorate the cake Make the frosting and spread over the cake, making deep swirls with a palette knife. Decorate with chocolate curls.

Chocolate layer cake

1 tablespoon cocoa powder
1 tablespoon hot water
175 g/6 oz butter or margarine, softened
175 g/6 oz castor sugar
3 eggs
175 g/6 oz self-raising flour
1½ teaspoons baking powder
Icing
225 g/8 oz chocolate butter icing (see page 112)
brandy (optional)
chocolate vermicelli
chocolate shapes (see page 121)

Blend together the cocoa powder and hot water. Allow to cool. Place all the ingredients for the cake in a mixing bowl and beat with a wooden spoon until well mixed. Divide the mixture between two bottom-lined and greased 18-cm/7-inch sandwich tins. Bake in a moderate oven (160°C, 325°F, Gas Mark 3) for 30–40 minutes. Turn out and cool on a wire tray.
To ice and decorate the cake Make the chocolate butter icing substituting brandy for the milk if liked. Use a little to sandwich the cakes together. Spread some icing around the sides of the cake and roll the sides in the vermicelli. Spread the top with some icing and mark a design using a serrated scraper. Using a greaseproof piping bag fitted with a star shaped nozzle, pipe a border around the edge. Decorate with chocolate shapes.

HELPFUL HINT
If you do not intend to eat this cake immediately, it will keep well un-iced in an airtight container. Once the cake is iced, it should be eaten as soon as possible.

HELPFUL HINT
To achieve the decoration on top of the cake, hold the scraper at an angle of about 45° to the cake and press just hard enough to indent a surface.

Cherry Madeira cake

175 g/6 oz butter or margarine
175 g/6 oz castor sugar
3 eggs
225 g/8 oz plain flour
½ teaspoon baking powder
175 g/6 oz glacé cherries, chopped
2 thin strips citron peel (optional)

Cream the butter and sugar together until light and fluffy. Beat in the eggs one at a time, adding a little of the flour with each egg after the first. Fold in the rest of the flour with the baking powder and cherries. Place in a lined and greased 1-kg/2-lb loaf tin, and arrange the peel over the centre. Bake in a moderate oven (160°C, 325°F, Gas Mark 3) for 1¼–1½ hours. Turn out and cool on a wire tray.

Variations
Ginger cake Add 2 teaspoons ground ginger and 50 g/2 oz chopped crystallised ginger to the mixture.

Coconut and lemon cake Add 50 g/2 oz desiccated coconut, the grated rind of 1 lemon and 2 tablespoons milk to the mixture.

Olde-fashioned Madeira cake

175 g/6 oz butter
175 g/6 oz castor sugar
grated rind of 1 lemon
3 eggs
225 g/8 oz plain flour
1½ teaspoons baking powder
2 tablespoons warm water
piece of candied peel

Cream the butter and sugar together until light and fluffy. Beat in the lemon rind. Beat in the eggs one at a time, adding a little of the flour with each egg after the first. Fold in the remaining flour and baking powder using a metal spoon. Gently fold in the water to give a soft, dropping consistency. Place in a bottom-lined and greased 18-cm/7-inch cake tin. Place the candied peel on the centre of the cake. Bake in a moderate oven (160°C, 325°F, Gas Mark 3) for 1¼–1½ hours. Allow to cool slightly in the tin before turning out and cooling on a wire tray.

HELPFUL HINT
This cake can also be made in an 18-cm/7-inch round cake tin and baked as above.

HELPFUL HINT
Brush the pieces of grated lemon rind from the grater with a dry pastry brush.

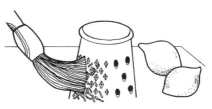

Gingerbread ring cake

125 g/4 oz butter or margarine
125 g/4 oz soft brown sugar
175 g/6 oz black treacle
225 g/8 oz plain flour
3–4 teaspoons ground ginger
½ teaspoon ground cinnamon
1 egg, beaten
½ teaspoon bicarbonate of soda
6 tablespoons milk
Icing and decoration
4 oz glacé icing (see page 114)
crystallised ginger

Melt the butter, sugar and treacle over a low heat until dissolved. Sieve the flour and spices into a bowl and pour in the melted mixture and egg. Dissolve the bicarbonate of soda in the milk and stir into the flour mixture, mixing well. Pour quickly into a greased and floured 20-cm/8-inch ring tin. Bake in a moderate oven (160°C, 325°F, Gas Mark 3) for 1–1¼ hours. Leave in the tin for a few minutes before turning out to cool on a wire tray.

To ice and decorate the cake Make the glacé icing and pour over the cake allowing it to run down the sides. Decorate with crystallised ginger.

Variations
Fruity gingerbread Add 75 g/3 oz raisins with the dry ingredients.

Orange gingerbread Add the coarsely grated rind of 2 oranges with the dry ingredients.

Traditional parkin

175 g/6 oz black treacle
175 g/6 oz butter or margarine
100 g/4 oz soft brown sugar
225 g/8 oz plain flour
2 teaspoons ground ginger
½ teaspoon grated nutmeg
¼ teaspoon ground cinnamon
1 teaspoon bicarbonate of soda
225 g/8 oz oatmeal
1 egg, beaten
150 ml/¼ pint milk

Place the treacle, butter and sugar in a saucepan and melt over a low heat. Allow to cool slightly. Place the flour, spices, bicarbonate of soda and oatmeal in a mixing bowl. Pour the melted mixture into the flour, then add the egg and milk, mixing together until smooth. Pour into a lined and greased 23-cm/9-inch square cake tin. Bake in a moderate oven (180°C, 350°F, Gas Mark 4) for 1¼–1½ hours. Leave to cool in the tin for a few minutes before turning out and cooling on a wire tray. Serve sliced and spread with butter.

HELPFUL HINT
To weigh the treacle without making a mess, first weigh the saucepan that it is to be cooked in, then weigh the treacle in it.

27

Yogurt cake

125 g/4 oz butter or margarine
125 g/4 oz castor sugar
3 eggs
2 teaspoons orange juice
1 (142-ml/5-fl oz) carton natural yogurt
100 g/4 oz ground almonds
150 g/5 oz self-raising flour
1 teaspoon baking powder
3 tablespoons cocoa powder
grated rind of 1 orange
Icing and decoration
350 g/12 oz orange butter icing (see page 112)
chocolate vermicelli
chocolate leaves (see page 120)
orange rind

Place all the ingredients in a mixing bowl and beat with a wooden spoon until well mixed. Place the mixture in two bottom-lined and greased 20-cm/8-inch sandwich tins. Bake in a moderate oven (160°C, 325°F, Gas Mark 3) for 40–45 minutes. Turn out and cool on a wire tray.

To ice and decorate the cake Make up the orange butter icing and use some to sandwich the cakes together. Spread some around the sides of the cake and roll in chocolate vermicelli. Spread a little of the remaining icing on top and pipe a border around the edge. Decorate with chocolate leaves and orange rind.

Honey Cake

125 g/4 oz butter or margarine
125 g/4 oz castor sugar
2 eggs
150 ml/¼ pint milk
175 g/6 oz honey
grated rind of 1 lemon
275 g/10 oz plain flour
1 teaspoon baking powder
½ teaspoon bicarbonate of soda
Filling
225 g/8 oz lemon butter icing (see page 112)
chopped walnuts
225 g/8 oz glacé icing (see page 114)
red food colouring

Cream the butter and sugar together until light and fluffy. Add the eggs one at a time, beating well. Gradually add the milk and honey and then fold in the grated lemon rind and dry ingredients. Place the mixture in two bottom-lined and greased 20-cm/8-inch sandwich tins. Bake in a moderate oven (180°C, 350°F, Gas Mark 4) for 35–40 minutes. Allow to cool before turning out on to a wire tray.

To ice and decorate the cake Make the butter icing and use a little to sandwich the cakes together. Spread some of the remaining icing around the sides of the cake and roll in the chopped walnuts. Using a grease-proof piping bag fitted with a star shaped nozzle, pipe a border of icing around the top edge of the cake.

Make the glacé icing and place 2 tablespoons in a small basin and colour pink. Spread the white glacé icing over the top of the cake and using a greaseproof piping bag with a small hole cut in the point, pipe a spiral design starting in the centre of the cake. Using a skewer, quickly drag it from the centre of the cake to the outer edges to give a feathered pattern. Allow to set.

Banana cake

100 g/4 oz butter or margarine
175 g/6 oz dark soft brown sugar
2 eggs
225 g/8 oz self-raising flour
grated rind of 1 lemon
50 g/2 oz glacé cherries, chopped
25 g/1 oz angelica, chopped
450 g/1 lb bananas (unpeeled weight) mashed
100 g/4 oz raisins
Icing and decoration
225 g/8 oz lemon glacé icing (see page 114)
sliced banana
lemon juice

Cream the butter and sugar together until light and fluffy. Beat in the eggs one at a time, adding a little of the flour with the second. Beat in the lemon rind and fold in the remaining ingredients. Place the mixture in a bottom-lined and greased 20-cm/8-inch cake tin. Bake in a moderate oven (180°C, 350°F, Gas Mark 4) for 1–1¼ hours. Turn out and cool on a wire tray.
To ice and decorate the cake Make the glacé icing and pour over the cake, allowing it to run down the sides. Decorate with slices of banana, dipped in lemon juice to prevent discoloration.

Cider apple cake

150 g/5 oz butter or margarine
150 g/5 oz castor sugar
2 eggs
225 g/8 oz plain flour
150 ml/¼ pint sweet cider
1 teaspoon baking powder
pinch of grated nutmeg
1 (35-g/1¼-oz) packet dehydrated apple flakes
Topping
2 red-skinned eating apples
sieved apricot jam

Cream the butter and sugar together until light and fluffy. Beat in the eggs one at a time, adding a little of the flour with the second. Gradually mix in the cider, alternating with the dry ingredients. Finally add the apple flakes. Place in a lined and greased 28 × 18-cm/11 × 7-inch Swiss roll tin and spread evenly. Bake in a moderate oven (180°C, 350°F, Gas Mark 4) for 45–50 minutes. Turn out and cool on a wire tray.
To decorate the cake Core and slice the apples very thinly and overlap in rows on top of the cake. Brush with the sieved apricot jam.

HELPFUL HINT
When glazing fruit with sieved apricot jam, add a little boiling water to the jam to give a smoother consistency.

Strawberry gâteau

Basic Genoese sponge
50 g/2 oz butter or margarine
75 g/3 oz castor sugar
3 eggs
75 g/3 oz plain flour
Filling and decoration
300 ml/½ pint double cream
225 g/8 oz strawberries
icing sugar

To make the basic Genoese sponge Melt the butter and allow to cool. Put the sugar and eggs into a large mixing bowl and place over a saucepan of hot water. Whisk until the mixture is thick and pale in colour and forms a trail when the whisk is lifted. Sieve the flour twice and fold into the whisked mixture together with the melted butter. Place in two bottom-lined and greased 18-cm/7-inch sandwich tins. Bake in a moderately hot oven (190°C, 375°F, Gas Mark 5) for 20–25 minutes. Turn out carefully and cool on a wire tray.

To fill and decorate the cake Lightly whip the cream and slice the strawberries. mix together one-third of the cream with some of the sliced fruit and use to spread over one of the cakes. Place the second cake on top. Spread some of the remaining cream over the top. Place the rest in a piping bag fitted with a star nozzle and pipe swirls around the top edge. Decorate with the remaining strawberries.

Swiss roll

50 g/2 oz castor sugar
2 eggs
50 g/2 oz plain flour
castor sugar
Filling and icing
3–4 tablespoons lemon curd
225 g/8 oz lemon butter icing (see page 112)
chocolate shapes (see page 121)

Place the sugar and eggs in a mixing bowl and whisk over a saucepan of hot water until the mixture is thick and pale in colour and forms a trail when lifted. Sieve the flour twice and fold into the mixture. Place the mixture in a lined and greased 28 × 18-cm/11 × 7-inch Swiss roll tin, smoothing over evenly. Bake in a moderately hot oven (200°C, 400°F, Gas Mark 6) for 8–10 minutes.

Meanwhile, place a damp teatowel on a working surface and lay a sheet of greaseproof paper on top. Sprinkle very lightly with castor sugar. Immediately the Swiss roll is cooked turn out on to the sugared paper. Remove the lining paper and trim the crusty edges. Make an indentation with a knife along the shortest edge nearest to you. Lay a sheet of clean greaseproof paper on top of the Swiss roll, then roll up tightly. Allow to cool.

To fill and decorate the roll Carefully unroll the Swiss roll. Remove the greaseproof paper, spread with the lemon curd and reroll. Make the butter icing and place in a piping bag fitted with a star nozzle. Pipe rows of icing along the roll and decorate with chocolate shapes.

HELPFUL HINT
To check if the sugar and egg mixture has been whisked sufficiently, raise the whisk from the bowl and allow mixture to pour off. If the thick mixture leaves a trail in the bowl, the flour may be added.

HELPFUL HINT
The Swiss roll can be filled with jam while still hot, then roll up and dredge with castor sugar.

Rich fruit cake

	12 cm/5 in ○ 10 cm/4 in □	15 cm/6 in ○ 12 cm/5 in □	18 cm/7 in ○ 15 cm/6 in □	20 cm/8 in ○ 18 cm/7 in □	23 cm/9 in ○ 20 cm/8 in □	25 cm/10 in ○ 23 cm/9 in □	28 cm/11 in ○ 25 cm/10 in □	30 cm/12 in ○ 28 cm/11 in □	32 cm/13 in ○ 30 cm/12 in □
BUTTER	65 g/2½ oz	75 g/3 oz	125 g/4 oz	150 g/5 oz	200 g/7 oz	250 g/9 oz	300 g/11 oz	375 g/13 oz	425 g/15 oz
DARK SOFT BROWN SUGAR	75 g/3 oz	90 g/3½ oz	150 g/5 oz	175 g/6 oz	225 g/8 oz	275 g/10 oz	350 g/12 oz	400 g/14 oz	450 g/1 lb
BLACK TREACLE	½ table-spoon	½ table-spoon	1 table-spoon	1 table-spoon	1 table-spoon	1 table-spoon	1½ table-spoons	2 table-spoons	2 table-spoons
EGGS	2	2	3	4	5	6	7	8	8
PLAIN FLOUR	75 g/3 oz	125 g/4 oz	175 g/6 oz	200 g/7 oz	250 g/9 oz	300 g/11 oz	400 g/14 oz	450 g/1 lb	525 g/ 1 lb 3 oz
GROUND MIXED SPICE	½ tea-spoon	½ tea-spoon	¾ tea-spoon	1 tea-spoon	1¼ tea-spoons	1½ tea-spoons	1½ tea-spoons	2 tea-spoons	2½ tea-spoons
GRATED NUTMEG	¼ tea-spoon	¼ tea-spoon	¼ tea-spoon	½ tea-spoon	½ tea-spoon	¾ tea-spoon	¾ tea-spoon	1 tea-spoon	1½ tea-spoons
GROUND ALMONDS	25 g/1 oz	25 g/1 oz	40 g/1½ oz	50 g/2 oz	65 g/2½ oz	75 g/3 oz	90 g/3½ oz	125 g/4 oz	140 g/4½ oz
GRATED LEMON RIND	½ lemon	½ lemon	1 lemon	1 lemon	1 lemon	2 lemons	2 lemons	2 lemons	2 lemons
GRATED ORANGE RIND	½ orange	½ orange	1 orange	1 orange	1 orange	2 oranges	2 oranges	2 oranges	3 oranges
CHOPPED ALMONDS	25 g/1 oz	40 g/1½ oz	50 g/2 oz	65 g/2½ oz	90 g/3½ oz	125 g/4 oz	150 g/5 oz	175 g/6 oz	200 g/7 oz
GLACÉ CHERRIES	25 g/1 oz	40 g/1½ oz	50 g/2 oz	65 g/2½ oz	90 g/3½ oz	125 g/4 oz	150 g/5 oz	175 g/6 oz	200 g/7 oz
RAISINS	25 g/1 oz	50 g/2 oz	75 g/3 oz	125 g/4 oz	150 g/5 oz	175 g/6 oz	200 g/7 oz	225 g/8 oz	250 g/9 oz
SULTANAS	75 g/3 oz	125 g/4 oz	150 g/5 oz	200 g/7 oz	250 g/9 oz	300 g/11 oz	375 g/13 oz	450 g/1 lb	525 g/ 1 lb 3 oz
CURRANTS	150 g/5 oz	175 g/6 oz	225 g/8 oz	275 g/10 oz	375 g/13 oz	450 g/1 lb	575 g/1¼ lb	675 g/1½ lb	800 g/1¾ lb
CHOPPED MIXED PEEL	25 g/1 oz	40 g/1½ oz	50 g/2 oz	65 g/2½ oz	90 g/3½ oz	125 g/4 oz	150 g/5 oz	175 g/6 oz	200 g/7 oz
BRANDY	1 table-spoon	1 table-spoon	1 table-spoon	2 table-spoons	2 table-spoons	3 table-spoons	3 table-spoons	4 table-spoons	4 table-spoons
ORANGE JUICE	1 table-spoon	1 table-spoon	1 table-spoon	1 table-spoon	2 table-spoons	2 table-spoons	3 table-spoons	3 table-spoons	3 table-spoons

This rich fruit cake is suitable for all types of special occasions, such as wedding, christening, Christmas and birthday cakes.

To keep the cake moist and give a good flavour, prick the base of the cooked, upturned cake with a skewer and pour over a little brandy. Stand on a wire tray for a few hours to allow the brandy to penetrate. Wrap the cake well and store in an airtight tin. It will keep for up to 6 months.

To make the fruit cake Cream the butter and sugar together until light and fluffy. Beat in the black treacle. Add the eggs one at a time, adding a little of the flour with each egg after the first. Mix the flour with all the remaining ingredients except the brandy and orange juice, and gradually fold into the creamed mixture. Stir in the brandy and orange juice. Place the mixture in a tin lined with double greaseproof paper and greased. Smooth the top of the cake using the back of a hot, wet metal spoon. Protect the outside of the tin with newspaper and bake in a cool oven (140°C, 275°F, Gas Mark 1). Check the cake after the first 3 hours, then at intervals after that. The smallest of the cakes should be checked after the first 2½ hours. (To test the cake, see pages 16 and 17.) Allow the cake to cool in the tin for 15 minutes before removing and cool on a wire tray.

Fruit 'n' nut cake

150 g/5 oz butter or margarine
6 tablespoons golden syrup
100 g/4 oz dried apricots
50 g/2 oz sultanas
225 g/8 oz raisins
100 g/4 oz currants
50 g/2 oz almonds, chopped
10 tablespoons milk
225 g/8 oz plain flour
pinch of grated nutmeg
grated rind of 1 orange
2 eggs
½ teaspoon bicarbonate of soda
Topping
50 g/2 oz dried apricots, chopped
50 g/2 oz whole almonds
25 g/1 oz glacé cherries
2 tablespoons honey

Place the butter, syrup, fruit, nuts and milk in a saucepan and melt over a low heat. Simmer gently for 5 minutes. Cool slightly. Place the flour, nutmeg and orange rind in a bowl and add the eggs. Stir the bicarbonate of soda into the cooled fruit mixture and add to the dry ingredients. Mix well and place in a lined and greased 18-cm/7-inch square cake tin. Smooth the surface and bake in a cool oven (150°C, 300°F, Gas Mark 2) for 1¾–2 hours. Turn out and cool on a wire tray.
To make the topping Place all the ingredients in a saucepan and heat until thoroughly mixed. Spread on top of the cake.

Farmhouse loaf

125 g/4 oz self-raising flour
125 g/4 oz plain wholemeal flour
pinch of grated nutmeg
½ teaspoon bicarbonate of soda
75 g/3 oz butter or margarine
125 g/4 oz castor sugar
50 g/2 oz raisins
25 g/1 oz glacé cherries
25 g/1 oz sultanas
25 g/1 oz chopped mixed peel
grated rind of 1 lemon
1 egg, beaten
6 tablespoons milk

Place the flours, nutmeg and bicarbonate of soda in a mixing bowl and rub in the butter until the mixture resembles fine breadcrumbs. Add the sugar, fruits, peel and lemon rind and mix in the eggs and milk to give a soft, dropping consistency. Place in a lined and greased 450-g/1-lb loaf tin. Bake in a moderate oven (180°C, 350°F, Gas Mark 4) for 50–60 minutes. Turn out and cool on a wire tray. Serve sliced and spread with butter.

HELPFUL HINT
A soft dropping consistency is achieved when a spoonful of mixture, when raised up from the bowl, drops slowly and easily from the spoon.

Dundee cake

225 g/8 oz butter or margarine
225 g/8 oz castor sugar
grated rind of 1 orange
5 eggs
300 g/11 oz plain flour
½ teaspoon baking powder
1 teaspoon ground mixed spice
pinch of grated nutmeg
225 g/8 oz currants
225 g/8 oz sultanas
225 g/8 oz raisins
50 g/2 oz glacé cherries, chopped
100 g/4 oz chopped mixed peel
Decoration
50 g/2 oz whole blanched almonds

Place all the ingredients in a mixing bowl and beat with a wooden spoon until well mixed. Place in a lined and greased 20-cm/8-inch cake tin and smooth the top with the back of a hot, wet metal spoon. Arrange the whole almonds in circles over the top. Bake in a cool oven (150°C, 300°F, Gas Mark 2) for 3½–4 hours. Leave to cool in the tin for 5 minutes, then turn out and finish cooling on a wire tray.

Note
Unblanched almonds are normally a little less expensive to purchase. To blanch them, place in a small bowl and pour on some boiling water. Leave for 2–3 minutes then take out one at a time and peel off the skins, which will come away easily.

Crystallised fruit cake

175 g/6 oz butter or margarine
175 g/6 oz soft brown sugar
3 eggs
225 g/8 oz plain flour
1 teaspoon ground mixed spice
grated rind of 1 orange
225 g/8 oz raisins
50 g/2 oz stem ginger, chopped
50 g/2 oz almonds, chopped
50 g/2 oz angelica, chopped
50 g/2 oz glacé cherries, chopped
50 g/2 oz brazil nuts, chopped
1–2 tablespoons orange juice
Decoration
crystallised ginger, whole almonds, brazil nuts,
glacé cherries
sieved apricot jam

Cream the butter and sugar together until light and fluffy. Beat in the eggs one at a time, adding a little of the sieved flour with each egg after the first. Fold in the remaining flour and spice with the orange rind, fruits and nuts, adding sufficient orange juice to give a soft dropping consistency.

Place in a lined and greased 18-cm/7-inch cake tin. Smooth the top with the back of a hot, wet metal spoon. Arrange rows of ginger, almonds, brazil nuts, and cherries on top of the cake. Bake in a cool oven (140°C, 275°F, Gas Mark 1) for 2½–3 hours. Allow to cool slightly before removing from the tin and placing on a wire tray. Glaze with warmed apricot jam while the cake is still warm.

HELPFUL HINT
To smooth the surface of a heavy cake mixture, spread over the surface with a metal spoon that has been dipped in hot water.

HELPFUL HINT
To prevent the bowl from slipping while the mixture is being creamed, place the bowl on a damp teatowel or sponge.

Boiled fruit cake

150 g/5 oz butter or margarine
generous 150 ml/¼ pint milk
6 tablespoons golden syrup
225 g/8 oz currants
225 g/8 oz raisins
100 g/4 oz sultanas
100 g/4 oz chopped mixed peel
100 g/4 oz dried apricots
225 g/8 oz plain flour
1 teaspoon ground mixed spice
pinch of grated nutmeg
2 eggs
½ teaspoon bicarbonate of soda

Place the butter, milk, syrup, dried fruits, peel and apricots in a saucepan and heat until the butter has melted. Simmer gently for 5 minutes then allow to cool slightly. Place the sieved flour and spices in a mixing bowl and add the eggs. Do not stir at this stage. Mix the bicarbonate of soda into the cooled fruit mixture and pour into the flour. Mix well and place in a lined and greased 18-cm/7-inch cake tin. Bake in a cool oven (150°C, 300°F, Gas Mark 2) for 1¾–2 hours. Turn out and cool on a wire tray.

Guinness cake

225 g/8 oz butter or margarine
225 g/8 oz soft brown sugar
4 eggs
275 g/10 oz plain flour
1 teaspoon ground mixed spice
pinch of grated nutmeg
225 g/8 oz raisins
225 g/8 oz sultanas
100 g/4 oz almonds
100 g/4 oz chopped mixed peel
grated rind of 1 lemon
150 ml/¼ pint Guinness to soak the cake

Cream the butter and sugar together until light and fluffy. Beat in the eggs one at a time, adding a little of the sieved flour with each egg after the first. Fold in the remaining ingredients until well mixed. Place in a lined and greased 18-cm/7-inch cake tin. Bake in a moderate oven (160°C, 325°F, Gas Mark 3) for 1 hour, then reduce to a cool oven (150°C, 300°F, Gas Mark 2) for a further 2¼–2½ hours.

Allow the cake to become cold before removing from the tin. Prick the base with a skewer and spoon over the Guinness. Allow to stand for 1 hour on a wire tray so the Guinness will penetrate, before wrapping.

Harvest fruit cake

175 g/6 oz butter or margarine
175 g/6 oz castor sugar
3 eggs
125 g/4 oz plain flour
150 g/5 oz self-raising flour
50 g/2 oz chopped mixed peel
50 g/2 oz glacé cherries, halved
175 g/6 oz mixed dried fruit
grated rind of 1 orange
5 tablespoons orange juice
crushed cube sugar

Cream the butter and sugar together until light and fluffy. Beat in the eggs one at a time, adding a little of the flour with each egg after the first. Toss the fruit in the remaining flour and fold into the mixture with the orange rind and juice. Place in a lined and greased 18-cm/7-inch cake tin and smooth the surface. Sprinkle with crushed sugar and bake in a moderate oven (160°C, 325°F, Gas Mark 3) for 1½–1¾ hours. Turn out and cool on a wire tray.

St Clements ring cake

175 g/6 oz butter or margarine
175 g/6 oz castor sugar
3 eggs
100 g/4 oz self-raising flour
50 g/2 oz ground almonds
grated rind of 1 orange
grated rind of 1 lemon
Icing and decoration
225 g/8 oz lemon glacé icing (see page 114)
shredded lemon and orange rind

Cream the butter and sugar together until light and fluffy. Beat in the eggs one at a time, adding a little of the sieved flour with each egg after the first. Fold in the remaining flour with the ground almonds and fruit rinds. Place the mixture in a greased and floured 20-cm/8-inch ring mould. Bake in a moderate oven (160°C, 325°F, Gas Mark 3) for 40–45 minutes. Turn out and cool on a wire tray.
To ice and decorate the cake Make the icing and pour over the cake allowing it to run down the sides. Decorate with shredded orange and lemon rind.

Butterscotch and lemon loaf

175 g/6 oz butter or margarine
175 g/6 oz soft brown sugar
3 eggs
grated rind of 1 lemon
225 g/8 oz self-raising flour
Icing and decoration
225 g/8 oz lemon butter icing (see page 112)
icing sugar to sprinkle
slices of fresh lemon
angelica leaves

Cream the butter and sugar together until light and fluffy. Beat in the eggs one at a time, adding a little of the sieved flour with each egg after the first. Beat in the lemon rind and then fold in the remaining flour with a metal spoon. Place in a bottom-lined and greased 1-kg/2-lb loaf tin. Bake in a moderate oven (180°C, 350°F, Gas Mark 4) for 40–45 minutes. Turn out and cool on a wire tray.
To ice and decorate the cake Make the icing. Cut the loaf cake horizontally into three layers. Sandwich together with half the butter icing. Dust the top of the cake with icing sugar and pipe rosettes down the centre with the remaining butter icing. Decorate with slices of lemon and angelica leaves. Using the blade of a knife mark diagonal lines on the icing sugar.

HELPFUL HINT
An easy way to fill a nylon piping bag is to insert the nozzle in the end and stand the bag in a round grater. Fold the edge back over the top edge of the grater. The butter icing can then be spooned in.

HELPFUL HINT
This cake freezes well un-iced. Place the cooled cake in a polythene bag, press out the air and secure with a twist tie. Label and freeze.

Chocolate and almond cake

175 g/6 oz butter or margarine
175 g/6 oz castor sugar
100 g/4 oz plain chocolate, melted
50 g/2 oz ground almonds
4 eggs, separated
50 g/2 oz self-raising flour
25 g/1 oz cornflour
Icing and decoration
225 g/8 oz chocolate butter icing (see page 112)
50 g/2 oz chopped almonds, toasted
few whole almonds, dipped in melted chocolate
few mimosa balls

Cream the butter and sugar together until light and fluffy. Beat in the melted chocolate, ground almonds and egg yolks. Fold in the flour and cornflour.

Whisk the egg whites until stiff, then carefully fold into the cake mixture. Divide the mixture between two bottom-lined and greased 20-cm/8-inch sandwich tins. Bake in a moderate oven (160°C, 325°F, Gas Mark 3) for 40–45 minutes. Turn out and cool on a wire tray.

To ice and decorate the cake Make the icing and use two-thirds to sandwich the cakes together and cover the sides. Roll the sides in the toasted almonds. Smooth the remaining icing over the surface and decorate with whole almonds half dipped in melted chocolate. Arrange the almonds to form flowers with a mimosa ball in the centre.

HELPFUL HINT
A quick and easy way to put the nuts on the side of the cake is to spread the sides with icing, then roll the cake over the nuts spread on a sheet of greaseproof paper.

Chocolate truffle cake

150 g/5 oz castor sugar
150 g/5 oz plain flour
2 tablespoons cocoa powder
2 teaspoons baking powder
5 tablespoons corn oil
5 tablespoons milk
1 tablespoon coffee essence
2 eggs, separated
75 g/3 oz plain chocolate
1 tablespoon brandy
25 g/1 oz butter
25 g/1 oz icing sugar
25 g/1 oz ground almonds
chocolate vermicelli
225 g/8 oz chocolate butter icing (see page 112)

Place the sugar, flour, cocoa powder and baking powder in a mixing bowl. Blend the oil, milk and coffee essence in a small basin. Add the egg yolks and mix well. Pour into the dry ingredients and beat well.

Whisk the egg whites until stiff, then fold into the mixture. Place the mixture in two greased and bottom-lined 18-cm/7-inch sandwich tins. Bake in a moderately hot oven (200°C, 400°F, Gas Mark 6) for 15–20 minutes. Turn out and cool on a wire tray.

To make the truffles Melt the chocolate in a basin over a saucepan of hot water. Stir in the brandy until well mixed. Remove from the heat and stir in the butter until melted. Add the sieved icing sugar and ground almonds. Leave in a cool place until firm. Divide into 10 and shape into balls. Toss in the chocolate vermicelli.

To ice and decorate the cake Sandwich the cakes together with a little of the butter icing. Spread some of the remaining icing around the sides of the cake and roll the sides in chocolate vermicelli. Spread the remaining icing over the top and arrange the truffles around the edge.

39

Aromatic teabread

100 g/4 oz dried peaches, chopped
300 g/12 oz self-raising flour
50 g/2 oz butter or margarine
75 g/3 oz castor sugar
1 tablespoon chopped fresh marjoram
1 tablespoon chopped fresh mint
grated rind of 1 lemon
100 g/4 oz almonds, chopped
2 eggs, beaten
7–8 tablespoons milk
Icing and decoration
225 g/8 oz lemon glacé icing (see page 114)
few sprigs of mint

Soak the dried peaches in water to cover overnight. Place the flour in a mixing bowl and rub in the butter. Add the sugar, herbs, lemon rind, drained peaches and almonds. Add the eggs and milk and mix to a soft dropping consistency. Place in a bottom-lined and greased 1-kg/2-lb loaf tin. Bake in a moderate oven (160°C, 325°F, Gas Mark 3) for 2–2¼ hours. Turn out and cool on a wire tray.

To ice and decorate the teabread Make the glacé icing and pour over the loaf allowing it to trickle down the sides, and decorate with sprigs of mint.

Raisin and bran teabread

225 g/8 oz raisins
75 g/3 oz bran
225 g/8 oz dark soft brown sugar
300 ml/½ pint milk
150 g/5 oz plain wholemeal flour
75 g/3 oz self-raising white flour
1 teaspoon baking powder
25 g/1 oz walnuts, chopped
Icing and decoration
100 g/4 oz glacé icing (see page 114)
toasted sunflower seeds to sprinkle

Place the raisins, bran, sugar and milk in a bowl and leave overnight. Stir the flours, baking powder and walnuts into the mixture. Place in a bottom-lined and greased 450-g/1-lb loaf tin. Bake in a moderately hot oven (190°C, 375°F, Gas Mark 5) for 1¼–1½ hours. Turn out and cool on a wire tray.

To ice and decorate the teabread Make up the glacé icing and pour over the top of the teabread. Sprinkle toasted sunflower seeds down the centre.

Brazilian teabread

125 g/4 oz raisins
125 g/4 oz sultanas
125 g/4 oz currants
125 g/4 oz glacé cherries
175 g/6 oz dark soft brown sugar
200 ml/7 fl oz strong black coffee
1 egg, beaten
250 g/9 oz plain flour
½ teaspoon bicarbonate of soda

Soak all the fruits and sugar overnight in the black coffee. Add the egg, flour and bicarbonate of soda and fold in carefully. Place in a lined and greased 1-kg/2-lb loaf tin and smooth the top evenly. Bake in a moderate oven (180°C, 350°F, Gas Mark 4) for 1½ hours. Allow to cool slightly in the tin, before turning out on to a wire tray. Slice and spread with butter.

This teabread improves with keeping.

Apricot and orange teabread

225 g/8 oz dried apricots
300 g/12 oz self-raising flour
50 g/2 oz butter or margarine
100 g/4 oz castor sugar
grated rind and juice of 1 orange
2 eggs
6 tablespoons milk
Icing and decoration
225 g/8 oz orange glacé icing (see page 114)
crystallised orange slices

Soak the apricots in water overnight. Drain well and chop finely. Place the flour in a mixing bowl and rub in the butter until the mixture resembles fine bread-crumbs. Stir in the sugar, chopped apricots, orange rind and juice, eggs and milk and mix until a soft, dropping consistency. Place in a bottom-lined and greased 1-kg/2-lb loaf tin. Bake in a moderate oven (160°C, 325°F, Gas Mark 3) for 1¼–1½ hours. Turn out and cool on a wire tray.

To ice and decorate the teabread Make the glacé icing and pour over the teabread. Decorate the top with the orange slices.

Variation

Substitute dried peaches (or a mixture of dried fruits) for the apricots. These can be purchased from super-markets and health food stores.

Malted teabread

50 g/2 oz dark soft brown sugar
25 g/1 oz butter or margarine
75 g/3 oz malt extract
225 g/8 oz plain wholemeal flour
2 teaspoons baking powder
100 g/4 oz mixed nuts, chopped
25 g/1 oz chopped mixed peel
150 ml/¼ pint milk
Glaze and decoration
50 g/2 oz sugar
4 tablespoons water
few mixed nuts, coarsely chopped

Place the sugar, butter and malt extract in a saucepan and melt over a low heat until dissolved. Allow to cool. Place the flour, baking powder, nuts and peel in a mixing bowl and make a well in the centre. Pour in the cooled mixture with the milk, and mix until a soft, dropping consistency. Place in a lined and greased 450-g/1-lb loaf tin. Bake in a moderate oven (160°C, 325°F, Gas Mark 3) for 1¼–1½ hours. Turn out and cool on a wire tray.

To make the glaze Dissolve the sugar in the water over a low heat, then simmer gently until syrupy. Brush over the hot teabread and sprinkle the top with chopped nuts.

HELPFUL HINT
To chop the fruit, hold the pointed end of a sharp knife down with one hand, keeping in place, and chop the fruit using the handle end only.

HELPFUL HINT
Malt can be purchased at any reputable chemist. For easy measuring, stand the jar in a saucepan of hot water before weighing to allow it to soften.

Chocolate pistachio loaf

125 g/4 oz self-raising flour
125 g/4 oz butter or margarine, softened
50 g/2 oz castor sugar
25 g/1 oz ground almonds
50 g/2 oz cocoa powder
50 g/2 oz plain chocolate, chopped
50 g/2 oz pistachio nuts, chopped
2 eggs
2 tablespoons milk
Icing and decoration
175 g/6 oz plain chocolate
knob of butter
few pistachio nuts, chopped

Place all the cake ingredients in a mixing bowl and beat with a wooden spoon until well mixed (2–3 minutes). Place the mixture in a lined and greased 450-g/1-lb loaf tin. Bake in a moderate oven (180°C, 350°F, Gas Mark 4) for 1¼–1½ hours. Turn out and cool on a wire tray.
To ice and decorate the loaf Melt the chocolate in a basin over a saucepan of hot water. Beat in a knob of butter to keep the chocolate shiny. Pour all over the loaf and sprinkle with chopped pistachio nuts.

Date and pineapple loaf

50 g/2 oz butter or margarine
225 g/8 oz stoned dates, chopped
50 g/2 oz light soft brown sugar
150 ml/¼ pint water
1 teaspoon bicarbonate of soda
50 g/2 oz glacé pineapple, chopped
1 egg, beaten
225 g/8 oz self-raising flour
Topping
2 tablespoons honey
25 g/1 oz glacé pineapple, chopped

Place the butter, dates, sugar and water in a saucepan and bring to the boil. Remove from the heat and allow to cool. Add the remaining ingredients and mix well together. Place in a lined and greased 1-kg/2-lb loaf tin and bake in a moderate oven (160°C, 325°F, Gas Mark 3) for 1¼–1½ hours. Turn out and cool on a wire tray.
To make the topping Melt the honey and brush over the top of the loaf. Sprinkle with the glacé pineapple.

HELPFUL HINT
If pistachio nuts are not available, nibbed almonds coloured with green food colouring can be substituted.

HELPFUL HINT
If glacé pineapple is not available crystallised ginger may be substituted.

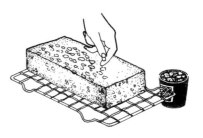

Spiced coffee teabread

225 g/8 oz self-raising flour
125 g/4 oz butter or margarine
125 g/4 oz dark soft brown sugar
3 tablespoons black coffee
75 g/3 oz walnuts, chopped
2 eggs
100 g/4 oz glacé cherries, chopped
½ teaspoon ground cinnamon
¼ teaspoon ground mixed spice
grated rind of 1 lemon

Place the flour in a mixing bowl and rub in the butter, until the mixture resembles fine breadcrumbs. Stir in the remaining ingredients. Place in a bottom-lined and greased 1-kg/2-lb loaf tin; bake in a moderate oven (180°C, 350°F, Gas Mark 4) for 1–1¼ hours. Turn out and cool on a wire tray. Serve sliced and spread with butter.

Minted chocolate marble loaf

125 g/4 oz butter or margarine
125 g/4 oz castor sugar
3 eggs
225 g/8 oz self-raising flour
2 tablespoons cocoa powder
2 tablespoons hot water
few drops of green food colouring
few drops of peppermint essence
Icing and decoration
225 g/8 oz chocolate fudge icing (see page 114)
minted chocolate sticks

Cream the butter and sugar together until light and fluffy. Beat in the eggs one at a time, adding a little of the flour with the second and third eggs. Fold in the remaining flour. Divide the mixture in half. Blend the cocoa powder with the hot water and add to one half. Colour the other half of the mixture green and flavour with peppermint essence. Place alternate spoonfuls of the mixtures in a lined and greased 1-kg/2-lb loaf tin. Bang the tin sharply on the table to level out the mixture. Bake in a moderate oven (160°C, 325°F, Gas Mark 3) for 1¼–1½ hours. Turn out and cool on a wire tray.
To ice and decorate the loaf Make up the icing and spread over the loaf. Decorate with the chocolate sticks.

HELPFUL HINT
When rubbing in the flour and butter, allow only the tips of fingers and thumbs to come into contact with the mixture. Lift the mixture high from the bowl to trap plenty of air.

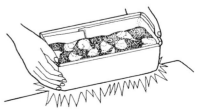

HELPFUL HINT
To obtain marble effect, place spoonfuls of the mixture at random into the loaf tin and bang the tin sharply on the table to level out the mixture.

Chapter

SMALL CAKES AND BISCUITS

Small cakes and biscuits are always in demand. For teas, parties and even as gifts, this chapter includes a delicious variety, from very simple crunchy coconut crisps to the more elaborate, yet easy, almond and orange puffs. Children will love the nutty brownies.

Fairy cakes

MAKES 18–20

**100 g/4 oz butter or margarine
100 g/4 oz castor sugar
2 eggs
150 g/5 oz self-raising flour
Icing and decoration
225 g/8 oz glacé icing (see page 114)
few drops of food colouring
small sweets or nuts**

Cream the butter and sugar together until pale and fluffy. Gradually beat in the eggs then sieve the flour over the mixture and fold in gently using a metal spoon. Place the mixture in greased patty tins or paper cake cases placed on a baking tray and bake in a moderate oven (180°C, 350°F, Gas Mark 4) for 15–20 minutes. Turn out of the patty tins and cool on a wire tray.

To ice and decorate the cakes Colour the glacé icing delicately in any preferred colour and use to cover the top of the cakes. The cakes may be feather iced using two different colours (see page 114) or may be decorated with various sweets or nuts as shown in the picture.

Variations

Chocolate cup cakes Add 2 tablespoons cocoa powder to the flour. Decorate the cakes with 175 g/6 oz melted plain chocolate or glacé icing with melted chocolate drizzled on top.

Nutty buns Add 50 g/2 oz chopped walnuts to the mixture. Decorate with glacé icing and halved walnuts.

Little fruit cakes Add 50 g/2 oz mixed dried fruit or chopped glacé cherries to the mixture. Mix 100 g/4 oz sieved icing sugar with 1–2 tablespoons sherry to give a smooth icing. Drizzle the icing over the top of the cakes.

Lemon maids

MAKES 18

Pastry
225 g/8 oz plain flour
100 g/4 oz butter or margarine
grated rind of 2 lemons
40 g/1½ oz castor sugar
1 tablespoon cold water
4 tablespoons lemon curd
Sponge topping
75 g/3 oz butter or margarine, softened
75 g/3 oz castor sugar
75 g/3 oz self-raising flour
25 g/1 oz ground almonds
1 egg, lightly beaten
3 tablespoons lemon juice
Icing and decoration
175 g/6 oz lemon curd
75 g/3 oz ground almonds
coarsely grated or pared lemon rind

To make the pastry Sieve the flour into a bowl, add the butter and rub in finely until the mixture resembles fine breadcrumbs. Add the lemon rind, sugar and water and mix to a smooth dough. Knead lightly then roll out thinly. Cut out eighteen 6–7.5-cm/2½–3-inch rounds and use to line patty tins. Place a little of the lemon curd in each pastry case then leave in a cool place while making the sponge topping.
To make the sponge topping Place all the ingredients for the topping in a bowl and beat well until pale and fluffy. Place enough of this mixture in each pastry case to reach almost to the top. Bake in a moderate oven (180°C, 350°F, Gas Mark 4) for approximately 20 minutes, until risen and golden. Turn out and cool on a wire tray.
To ice and decorate the cakes Mix the lemon curd with the ground almonds and spread over the cooled cakes. Decorate with a little lemon rind.

Minty chocolate cups

MAKES 24

125 g/4 oz butter or margarine
125 g/4 oz castor sugar
¼ teaspoon peppermint essence
2 eggs, lightly beaten
125 g/4 oz self-raising flour
125 g/4 oz plain chocolate, grated
Icing and decoration
225 g/8 oz plain chocolate, melted
crystallised mint leaves (see page 122)

Cream the butter with the sugar until light and fluffy. Gradually beat in the peppermint essence and eggs. Sieve the flour over the mixture and fold in using a metal spoon. Lastly fold in the grated chocolate. Divide the mixture between 24 paper cake cases placed on a baking tray or in patty tins and bake in a moderately hot oven (190°C, 375°F, Gas Mark 5) for 20 minutes. Cool on a wire tray.
To ice and decorate the cakes When cold, spread the tops of the cakes with melted chocolate and decorate with a few crystallised mint leaves. The cakes may be served in their paper cases or with the cases removed.

HELPFUL HINT
To melt the chocolate, place in a basin over a saucepan of hot water.

Apple and ginger rings

MAKES 9

2 eggs
100 g/4 oz golden syrup
1 medium cooking apple (approximately
175 g/6 oz)
juice of 1 lemon
1 piece preserved ginger, chopped
100 g/4 oz self-raising flour
¼ teaspoon ground ginger
Icing and decoration
100 g/4 oz icing sugar
1–2 tablespoons ginger wine
crystallised ginger
few slices of apple, dipped in lemon juice

Whisk the eggs with the syrup until pale and thick. Peel, core and grate the apple, sprinkle with the lemon juice and mix with the preserved ginger. Fold this apple mixture into the eggs. Sieve the flour and ground ginger together and fold into the egg mixture.

Divide the mixture between nine well greased 11-cm/4½-inch ring tins and bake in a moderately hot oven (190°C, 375°F, Gas Mark 5) for 20–25 minutes. Turn out and cool on a wire tray.

To ice and decorate the rings Sieve the icing sugar into a bowl and mix to a smooth consistency with the ginger wine. Drizzle the icing over the cooled cakes and decorate with crystallised ginger and small pieces of apple.

Nutty angelica fancies

MAKES 12

125 g/4 oz butter or margarine
125 g/4 oz castor sugar
2 eggs, lightly beaten
125 g/4 oz self-raising flour, sieved
125 g/4 oz walnuts, chopped
75 g/3 oz angelica, chopped
Icing and decoration
225 g/8 oz glacé icing (see page 114)
25 g/1 oz walnuts, chopped
50 g/2 oz angelica, chopped

Cream the butter with the sugar until light and fluffy. Gradually beat in the eggs and fold in the flour using a metal spoon. Mix together the walnuts and angelica and fold into the cake mixture. Divide the mixture between 12 greased dariole moulds and bake in a moderate oven (180°C, 350°F, Gas Mark 4) for 25–30 minutes. Turn out and cool on a wire tray.

To ice and decorate the cakes Drizzle the glacé icing over the top of each cake and sprinkle with a mixture of chopped walnuts and angelica.

HELPFUL HINT
To prevent fruit from discolouring, slice with a stainless steel knife and sprinkle with lemon juice.

HELPFUL HINT
Place the filled dariole moulds on a baking tray to ease the lifting in and out of the oven.

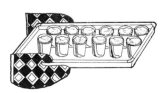

Florentines

MAKES 16–18

50 g/2 oz soft brown sugar
2 tablespoons golden syrup
50 g/2 oz butter or margarine
25 g/1 oz walnuts, chopped
25 g/1 oz glacé cherries, chopped
25 g/1 oz raisins, chopped
grated rind of 1 orange
grated rind of 1 lemon
40 g/1½ oz plain flour
Decoration
175 g/6 oz plain chocolate, melted

Place the sugar, syrup and butter in a saucepan and stir over a gentle heat until melted and well combined. Add the nuts, fruit and fruit rind then stir in the flour. Place teaspoonfuls of the mixture well apart on greased baking trays and bake in a moderate oven (180°C, 350°F, Gas Mark 4) for 8–10 minutes or until golden in colour and well spread. Cool slightly on the baking tray then carefully remove to a wire tray and leave until cold.

To decorate the florentines Spread the smooth sides with melted chocolate. Mark with a fork when the chocolate is almost set.

Brandy snaps

MAKES 20

50 g/2 oz butter
2 tablespoons golden syrup
50 g/2 oz soft brown sugar
50 g/2 oz plain flour
Filling
300 ml/½ pint double cream
1 tablespoon castor sugar
2 tablespoons brandy

Place the butter, syrup and sugar in a saucepan. Stir over a gentle heat until melted and well combined then sieve the flour and stir in well. Place teaspoonfuls of the mixture well apart on greased baking trays and bake in a moderately hot oven (190°C, 375°F, Gas Mark 5) for 5–8 minutes. Cool slightly on the baking trays then carefully remove using a palette knife and wrap around greased handles of wooden spoons. Leave until cold then carefully slide off.

To fill the brandy snaps Whip the cream with the sugar and brandy. Place in a piping bag fitted with a star nozzle and pipe the cream into the biscuits. Serve immediately.

Variations

Almond tuiles To the basic biscuit mixture add 50 g/2 oz flaked almonds. Bake and cool slightly as above then carefully remove the biscuits from the baking tray with a palette knife and wrap over the top of a greased rolling pin. Carefully slide off when cool.

Biscuit cups Carefully shape the cooked and slightly cooled biscuits into greased patty tins to form little cups. Remove the cooled biscuits and serve filled with fresh summer fruits, homemade ice creams or sorbets and whipped cream.

HELPFUL HINT
If the florentines become too difficult to remove from the trays place the baking tray back into the warm oven just to soften the mixture.

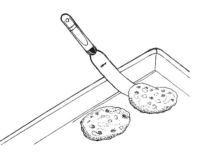

HELPFUL HINT
To curve the tuiles, wrap the warm biscuits over the top of a greased rolling pin and slide off when cool.

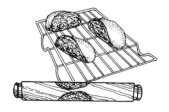

Mocha rounds

MAKES 20–24 SLICES

75 g/3 oz golden syrup
50 g/2 oz butter
grated rind of 1 orange and juice of ½ orange
grated rind of 1 lemon
75 g/3 oz sultanas
100 g/4 oz glacé cherries, roughly chopped
2 teaspoons coffee essence
2 tablespoons ginger wine
75 g/3 oz blanched almonds, chopped
225 g/8 oz plain chocolate digestive biscuits,
crushed
75 g/3 oz ground almonds
Coating
100 g/4 oz blanched almonds, chopped

Place all the ingredients, except the biscuits and ground almonds in a saucepan over a low heat. Stir continuously until completely melted and combined then bring to the boil and cook for 1 minute. Stir in the digestive biscuits and ground almonds and leave in a cool place until firm enough to shape into a long roll, approximately 5 cm/2 inches in diameter and 23–25 cm/9–10 inches in length.

To coat the roll Roll in the chopped blanched almonds until completely coated. Wrap in foil or cling film and chill until quite firm. Cut into slices before serving.

Coconut fudge slices

MAKES 20–24

250 g/9 oz butter
100 g/4 oz icing sugar, sieved
175 g/6 oz coconut flour
225 g/8 oz plain flour
Topping and decoration
175 g/6 oz sugar
50 g/2 oz butter
250 ml/8 fl oz milk
50 g/2 oz desiccated coconut
50 g/2 oz plain chocolate, melted

Cream the butter with the icing sugar until pale and very fluffy. Gradually beat in the coconut flour and flour then knead to a smooth, soft dough. Line and grease a 28 × 18-cm/11 × 7-inch Swiss roll tin and press the biscuit mixture evenly into it. Prick all over with a fork and chill for 30 minutes before baking in a moderate oven (160°C, 325°F, Gas Mark 3) for 40–45 minutes, until pale golden in colour.

To make the topping Place the sugar, butter and milk in a saucepan and bring to the boil, stirring continuously. Continue to boil, stirring occasionally to prevent sticking, until the mixture is reduced to about half its original volume and is thick and creamy. Remove from the heat, add the coconut and beat thoroughly. Spread over the slice and cut into fingers. Chill.

To decorate the slices Place the melted chocolate in a greaseproof piping bag with a tiny hole cut in the point. Remove the slices from the tin and pipe the chocolate in a pattern down the centre of each slice.

Ginger drops

MAKES 20–24

1 tablespoon black treacle
50 g/2 oz golden syrup
75 g/3 oz muscovado sugar or dark soft brown
sugar
75 g/3 oz butter or margarine
50 g/2 oz chopped mixed peel
1 piece preserved ginger, chopped
175 g/6 oz plain flour
1 teaspoon ground ginger
Decoration
100 g/4 oz plain chocolate, melted
icing sugar

Place the treacle, syrup, sugar, butter, peel and ginger
in a saucepan and melt over a low heat, stirring
continuously. Sieve the flour and ginger over the
slightly cooled mixture then beat well until smooth.
Cool slightly until the mixture is easily formed into
small balls the size of walnuts. Flatten the balls slightly
and place well apart on greased baking trays. Bake in a
moderate oven (180°C, 350°F, Gas Mark 4) for 15
minutes. Allow to cool for a minute on the baking tray
then transfer to a wire tray and leave until quite cold.
To decorate the biscuits Dip half of each biscuit in the
melted chocolate and leave on oiled greaseproof
paper until dry. Use a small piece of greaseproof paper
to cover the chocolate side of the biscuits and sieve the
remaining half with a little icing sugar.

Sesame flapjack

MAKES 12 PIECES

100 g/4 oz thick honey
50 g/2 oz golden syrup
100 g/4 oz butter or margarine
grated rind of 1 orange
100 g/4 oz stoned dates, chopped
50 g/2 oz sesame seeds
225 g/8 oz rolled oats
Topping
50 g/2 oz sesame seeds
2 tablespoons thick honey

Melt the honey, syrup and butter together. Add the
orange rind, dates, sesame seeds and oats and stir
well. Line a 24 × 15-cm/9½ × 6-inch shallow, oblong
tin with rice paper and press the mixture into it. Bake in
a moderate oven (180°C, 350°F, Gas Mark 4) for 20
minutes.
To make the topping Mix the sesame seeds with the
honey and warm over a saucepan of hot water until
the mixture is soft enough to spread easily. Remove
the flapjack from the oven and spread the topping
evenly over it. Return to the oven and bake for a
further 10–15 minutes, or until golden in colour. Allow
to cool in the tin and cut into 12 pieces while still warm.

Almond and orange puffs

MAKES 12

150 ml/¼ pint water
50 g/2 oz butter
65 g/2½ oz plain flour, sieved
2 eggs
grated rind of 1 orange
50 g/2 oz flaked almonds
Filling and icing
300 ml/½ pint double cream
2 tablespoons castor sugar
grated rind of 1 orange and juice of ½ orange
100 g/4 oz orange glacé icing (see page 114)
toasted flaked almonds

Heat the water and butter together in a saucepan until the butter has completely melted then bring rapidly to the boil. Remove from the heat and add all the flour. Return to the heat and beat until the mixture forms a smooth ball which leaves the sides of the pan quite clean. Allow to cool until just warm.

Add the eggs individually and beat in thoroughly together with the orange rind to give a smooth soft paste. Stir in the flaked almonds. Place heaps of the mixture (about 2 teaspoonfuls each in size) well apart on greased baking trays. Bake in a hot oven (220°C, 425°F, Gas Mark 7) for 10 minutes then reduce to moderately hot (190°C, 375°F, Gas Mark 5) and bake for a further 15 minutes. Make a small slit in the puffs immediately they are removed from the oven. Cool on a wire tray.

To fill and ice the puffs Whip the cream with the sugar, orange rind and juice until stiff. Fill the buns using a teaspoon or a piping bag fitted with a large plain nozzle. Make the glacé icing and drizzle over the top of the buns then sprinkle with toasted flaked almonds.

Meringues

MAKES 12–13 pairs

2 egg whites
100 g/4 oz castor sugar
Filling and decoration
300 ml/½ pint double cream
few glacé cherries
angelica leaves

Whisk the egg whites until stiff. Gradually whisk in half the sugar then carefully fold in the remainder using a metal spoon. Transfer the mixture to a piping bag fitted with a large star nozzle and pipe small meringues on to greased baking trays. Dry out in a very cool oven (110°C, 225°F, Gas Mark ¼), or at the lowest setting to which the oven may be turned, for 3½–4 hours. Remove and cool on a wire tray.

To fill and decorate the meringues Whip the cream until stiff and use to sandwich the meringues together, either by piping through a larger star nozzle or by using a spoon. Decorate with pieces of cherry and angelica leaves.

Variations

Lemon meringues When folding in the last of the sugar, add the grated rind of 1 large or 2 small lemons and fold in carefully. Decorate the finished, sandwiched meringues with small pieces of fresh lemon and angelica leaves.

Orange meringues Fold in the grated rind of 1 orange together with the last of the sugar. Decorate the finished, sandwiched meringues with leaf shapes cut from pared orange peel.

Chocolate shortbread hearts

MAKES 22–24

175 g/6 oz butter
75 g/3 oz castor sugar
225 g/8 oz plain flour
25 g/1 oz cocoa powder
Icing and decoration
100 g/4 oz chocolate butter icing (see page 112)
175 g/6 oz plain chocolate, melted

Cream the butter and sugar together until pale and fluffy. Sieve the flour with the cocoa powder and beat into the creamed mixture to give a soft dough. Chill, knead lightly and roll out thinly. Use a heart-shaped biscuit cutter to cut out the biscuits and place on greased baking trays. Bake in a moderate oven (160°C, 325°F, Gas Mark 3) for 15 minutes. Cool slightly on the baking trays then remove to wire trays and leave until cold.

To ice and decorate the biscuits Use a small star nozzle to pipe around the edge of the biscuits with chocolate butter icing. Carefully pour the melted chocolate into the centre of the biscuits and allow to cool.

55

Honey squares

MAKES 12

175 g/6 oz thick honey
175 g/6 oz butter or margarine
75 g/3 oz demerara sugar
100 g/4 oz sultanas
75 g/3 oz blanched almonds, chopped
grated rind of 2 oranges
juice of ½ orange
2 eggs, lightly beaten
200 g/7 oz self-raising flour
1 teaspoon baking powder
½ teaspoon ground cinnamon
Topping
100 g/4 oz blanched almonds
5 tablespoons thick honey
50 g/2 oz sultanas
generous pinch of cinnamon
grated rind of 1 orange

Melt the honey, butter and sugar together with the sultanas, almonds, orange rind and juice over a gentle heat. Cool slightly. Beat in the eggs. Sieve together the dry ingredients and beat into the mixture to give a smooth batter.

Pour into a lined and greased 18- x 26-cm/7- x 10½-inch shallow tin and bake in a moderate oven (160°C, 325°F, Gas Mark 3) for 40–50 minutes. Cool slightly in the tin then mix together all the ingredients for the topping. Warm slightly if necessary then spread over the top of the cake and leave to cool. Cut into squares when cold.

Lemon honey buns

MAKES 12–14

100 g/4 oz butter or margarine
50 g/2 oz soft brown sugar
100 g/4 oz thick honey
grated rind and juice of 1 lemon
2 eggs, lightly beaten
225 g/8 oz self-raising flour
1 teaspoon baking powder
Icing and decoration
225 g/8 oz lemon glacé icing (see page 114)
pared lemon rind

Melt the butter, sugar and honey together with the lemon rind and juice over a gentle heat, stirring occasionally. Leave to cool slightly. Beat in the eggs. Sift the flour and baking powder together and beat thoroughly into the melted mixture to give a smooth thick batter.

Divide between greased, deep patty tins and bake in a moderately hot oven (190°C, 375°F, Gas Mark 5) for 15–20 minutes. Cool on a wire tray.

Decorate with glacé icing and pieces of pared lemon rind.

HELPFUL HINT
*When weighing honey,
first lightly flour the scale
pan and then spoon in
the ingredient. It can then
be easily transferred to
the saucepan leaving a
clean scale pan.*

Crunchy coffee cakes

MAKES 18–20

Base and topping
100 g/4 oz plain flour
50 g/2 oz butter or margarine
75 g/3 oz soft brown sugar
100 g/4 oz brazil nuts, chopped
Cake mixture
100 g/4 oz butter or margarine
100 g/4 oz castor sugar
2 eggs
100 g/4 oz self-raising flour
2 tablespoons instant coffee granules

Sieve the flour into a bowl and rub in the butter until the mixture resembles fine breadcrumbs. Add the sugar and chopped nuts and stir together well. Press half of this mixture over the base of a greased 28 × 18-cm/11 × 7-inch Swiss roll tin.

To make the cake mixture Cream the butter with the sugar until pale and fluffy. Beat in the eggs and sieve the flour over the mixture. Fold in lightly using a metal spoon. Lastly, lightly stir in the instant coffee granules. Spread this mixture evenly over the base and sprinkle the remaining nut mixture on top. Bake in a moderate oven (160°C, 325°F, Gas Mark 3) for approximately 1 hour, or until golden brown in colour and firm to the touch. Leave to cool in the tin then cut into pieces and carefully remove from the tin.

Chocolate marble squares

MAKES 25

175 g/6 oz butter or margarine
175 g/6 oz castor sugar
3 eggs
175 g/6 oz self-raising flour
¼ teaspoon almond essence
2 tablespoons cocoa powder
2 tablespoons boiling water
Icing and decoration
225 g/8 oz glacé icing (see page 114)
few drops of almond essence
chocolate curls (see page 120)

Cream the butter with the sugar until pale and fluffy. Gradually beat in the eggs then sieve the flour and fold in carefully using a metal spoon. Divide the mixture in half and flavour one portion with the almond essence. Cream the cocoa powder with the boiling water, cool slightly and beat into the other portion of cake mixture.

Place small spoonfuls of the mixture at random in a lined and greased 25-cm/10-inch square shallow tin and swirl the two mixtures together slightly. Bang the tin sharply on the table to even out the mixture and bake in a moderate oven (160°C, 325°F, Gas Mark 3) for 1 hour 5 minutes, or until risen and firm to the touch. Turn out, remove the lining paper and cool on a wire tray.

To ice and decorate the squares Cut the cake into 25 squares. Flavour the glacé icing with a few drops of almond essence and spread over the top of the squares. Decorate with chocolate curls.

Spiced peanut bars

MAKES 32

100 g/4 oz golden syrup
100 g/4 oz butter or margarine
225 g/8 oz unsalted peanuts, chopped
2 eggs
175 g/6 oz self-raising flour
½ teaspoon ground allspice
½ teaspoon ground cinnamon
generous pinch of grated nutmeg
pinch of salt
grated rind of 1 orange
Topping
2 tablespoons golden syrup
50 g/2 oz peanut butter
50 g/2 oz unsalted peanuts, chopped
generous pinch of ground cinnamon
2 tablespoons orange juice

Melt the golden syrup with the butter, add the peanuts and allow to cool slightly then beat in the eggs. Sieve the flour with the spices and salt then beat into the peanut mixture together with the orange rind. Spread evenly in a bottom-lined and greased 25-cm/10-inch square, shallow tin. Bake in a moderate oven (180°C, 350°F, Gas Mark 4) for 25–30 minutes.
To make the topping Mix together all the ingredients for the topping and warm over a gentle heat. Spread the topping over the cake immediately it comes out of the oven then allow to cool in the tin. Cut into bars when cold.

HELPFUL HINT
Children will enjoy these as an extra for the luncheon box as they are filling and nutritious.

Nutty fruit round

MAKES 8

50 g/2 oz sultanas
50 g/2 oz raisins
25 g/1 oz currants
25 g/1 oz chopped mixed peel
50 g/2 oz glacé cherries, roughly chopped
grated rind and juice of 1 orange
2 tablespoons rum
75 g/3 oz golden syrup
75 g/3 oz walnuts, chopped
1 egg
50 g/2 oz wheatgerm
75 g/3 oz plain wholewheat flour
½ teaspoon baking powder
Icing and decoration
100 g/4 oz icing sugar
1–2 tablespoons rum

Combine the sultanas, raisins, currants, peel and cherries. Add the orange rind and juice, rum and syrup then heat slowly until boiling. Allow to cool slightly then add the nuts and beat in the egg. Mix the wheatgerm with the flour and baking powder and beat thoroughly into the fruit mixture.

Spread evenly into a lined and greased 23-cm/9-inch sandwich tin and bake in a moderate oven (180°C, 350°F, Gas Mark 4) for 30–40 minutes. Allow to cool in the tin. When cold, carefully turn out on to a plate and remove the greaseproof paper. Invert the cake on to a serving plate.
To ice and decorate the round Sieve the icing sugar into a bowl and beat in the rum to give a smooth glacé icing. Drizzle over the top of the cake, and cut into eight wedges when almost set.

Coconut crisps

MAKES 12

**1 egg white
50 g/2 oz castor sugar
100 g/4 oz desiccated coconut
few glacé cherries, sliced**

Whisk the egg white until stiff then gradually whisk in all the sugar until thick and glossy. Stir in the coconut to give a stiff mixture. Using wet hands, shape into 12 balls about the size of walnuts and place on greased baking trays. Bake in a moderate oven (180°C, 350°F, Gas Mark 4) for 15–20 minutes, until golden in colour and firm to the touch. Remove and cool on a wire tray. Decorate each cake with a slice of glacé cherry.

Brownies

MAKES 16–18

**50 g/2 oz self-raising flour
½ teaspoon baking powder
40 g/1½ oz cocoa powder
25 g/1 oz ground almonds
225 g/8 oz soft brown sugar
grated rind of 1 orange
100 g/4 oz butter or margarine, softened
2 eggs, lightly beaten
Icing
100 g/4 oz plain chocolate
25 g/1 oz butter or margarine
50 g/2 oz blanched almonds, chopped**

Sieve the flour, baking powder and cocoa powder into a bowl. Add the ground almonds, sugar and orange rind and mix together well. Beat the butter and eggs into the dry ingredients until smooth. Spread evenly into a lined and greased 18-cm/7-inch square, shallow tin. Bake in a moderate oven (160°C, 325°F, Gas Mark 3) for 50–55 minutes. Allow to cool in the tin. **To ice the brownies** Melt the chocolate with the butter then stir in the chopped almonds. Spread evenly over the brownies then cut into small squares when half set.

HELPFUL HINT
These little cakes make an attractive present. Place them in small paper cases and arrange in a box or tray. Tie a ribbon around the box before presenting the gift.

HELPFUL HINT
Brownies freeze well un-iced. Interleave the squares with waxed paper, wrap, label and freeze.

Banana date fingers

MAKES 18

100 g/4 oz butter or margarine
50 g/2 oz castor sugar
1 egg yolk
100 g/4 oz self-raising flour
100 g/4 oz ground almonds
Filling
4 bananas (about 675 g/1½ lb unpeeled weight)
juice of 1 lemon
225 g/8 oz dates, stoned and halved
50 g/2 oz blanched almonds, halved
3 tablespoons soft brown sugar
Topping
1 egg
50 g/2 oz soft brown sugar
25 g/1 oz plain flour
50 g/2 oz ground almonds
icing sugar

Cream the butter with the sugar until pale and fluffy. Beat in the egg yolk then stir in the flour and ground almonds to form a very soft dough. Press into the base of a greased 18 × 28-cm/7 × 11-inch Swiss roll tin and prick all over with a fork. Bake blind in a moderately hot oven (160°C, 325°F, Gas Mark 3) for 30–40 minutes. Cool slightly.
To make the filling Slice the bananas and sprinkle with the lemon juice, mixing well. Add the remaining ingredients. Stir well and arrange evenly over the base.
To make the topping Whisk the egg with the sugar until thick and creamy. Sieve the flour over the egg mixture and fold in carefully with the ground almonds. Spread this mixture thinly and evenly over the bananas and dates. Bake in a moderately hot oven (190°C, 375°F, Gas Mark 5) for 40 minutes, until golden in colour. Cool in the tin and cut into fingers when cold. Sieve icing sugar over the tops before serving.

Fruity bran fingers

MAKES 16

grated rind and juice of 2 oranges
grated rind of 1 lemon
50 g/2 oz clear honey
2 tablespoons sherry
50 g/2 oz butter, melted
100 g/4 oz All-Bran
100 g/4 oz dried figs, chopped
100 g/4 oz sultanas
50 g/2 oz flaked almonds
50 g/2 oz glacé cherries, chopped
Icing and decoration
75 g/3 oz plain chocolate, melted
25 g/1 oz butter, melted
50 g/2 oz blanched almonds, chopped

Mix together the fruit rinds and juice, honey, sherry and butter. Combine the All-Bran, figs, sultanas, almonds and cherries then pour over the wet ingredients and mix together thoroughly. Press into a greased shallow oblong tin measuring 15 × 24 cm/6 × 9½ inches.
To ice and decorate the fingers Mix the melted chocolate with the melted butter and spread evenly over the top of the fruit mixture. Sprinkle with chopped almonds and leave in a cool place until quite firm, preferably overnight. Cut into fingers and carefully remove from the tin.

Variation
For an exciting addition to children's parties, cut the un-iced mixture into cubes, put on the end of cocktail sticks and dip into melted chocolate. Stick into an orange or grapefruit.

Cinnamon rings

MAKES 24

175 g/6 oz plain flour
100 g/4 oz butter or margarine
50 g/2 oz castor sugar
½ teaspoon ground cinnamon
grated rind of 1 orange
1 egg yolk
Icing and decoration
225 g/8 oz orange glacé icing (see page 114)
coarsely grated orange rind

Sieve the flour into a bowl and rub in the butter until the mixture resembles fine breadcrumbs. Add the sugar, cinnamon, orange rind and egg yolk then mix to form a smooth dough. Knead lightly then roll out thinly. Use a 6-cm/2½-inch fluted biscuit cutter to cut out the biscuits. Cut the middle out of each biscuit by using a 2.5-cm/1-inch fluted cutter. Knead the trimmings together, re-roll and cut out. Place on greased baking trays and bake in a moderate oven (180°C, 350°F, Gas Mark 4) for 10–15 minutes. Cool on a wire tray.
To ice and decorate the rings Carefully coat the top of the biscuits with orange glacé icing and sprinkle with coarsely grated orange rind.

Variation
Any left over centres of the rings can be baked separately as small biscuits and served at a children's party.

Walnut coffee trumpets

MAKES 20

50 g/2 oz butter or margarine
25 g/1 oz golden syrup
50 g/2 oz soft brown sugar
50 g/2 oz walnuts, chopped
40 g/1½ oz plain flour
Filling
300 ml/½ pint double cream
2 tablespoons golden syrup
1 tablespoon coffee essence

Place the butter, syrup and sugar in a saucepan and stir over a gentle heat until melted and well combined. Stir in the nuts and flour. Place teaspoonfuls of this mixture on to greased baking trays and bake in a moderate oven (180°C, 350°F, Gas Mark 4) for 8–10 minutes until well spread, bubbling and a dark golden colour. Allow to cool on the trays for a minute then carefully remove using a palette knife and wrap around greased cream horn tins. Leave on a wire tray until cool then carefully remove the tins.
To fill the trumpets Whip the cream with the syrup until thick then stir in the coffee essence. Spoon or pipe the cream into the horns and serve immediately.

HELPFUL HINT
These biscuits may be stored unfilled for 2–3 weeks in an airtight container and make an ideal accompaniment to cold desserts.

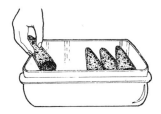

Fruity Oatcakes

MAKES 20–24

100 g/4 oz butter or margarine
100 g/4 oz soft brown sugar
grated rind of 1 orange
grated rind of 1 lemon
50 g/2 oz plain flour
175 g/6 oz pinhead oatmeal
50 g/2 oz rolled oats
pinch of bicarbonate of soda
pinch of salt
1 egg yolk

Cream the butter with the sugar and fruit rinds until soft and fluffy. Stir together the remaining dry ingredients. Beat the egg yolk into the creamed mixture then gradually stir in the dry ingredients to form a soft dough. Knead lightly and roll out thinly. Use a 5-cm/2-inch biscuit cutter to cut out the biscuits. Place well apart on greased baking trays and bake in a moderate oven (180°C, 350°F, Gas Mark 4) for 10–15 minutes. Cool slightly on the baking trays then transfer to a wire tray and leave to cool.

Variation
To make *Traditional oatcakes*, to serve with cheese omit the sugar and grated fruit rinds from the recipe. The butter should then be rubbed into the dry ingredients and mixed to a dough with the egg yolk. Cook in a moderate oven (180°C, 350°F, Gas Mark 4) for 15–20 minutes.

Peanut cookies

MAKES 12–15

50 g/2 oz butter or margarine, softened
50 g/2 oz soft brown sugar
50 g/2 oz salted peanuts, roughly chopped
grated rind of 1 orange
75 g/3 oz self-raising flour
1 tablespoon orange juice

Cream the butter with the sugar until light and fluffy. Mix in all the remaining ingredients to form a soft dough. Take small pieces of dough, about the size of a walnut, and roll into a ball. Place well apart on greased baking trays, flatten with a fork and bake in a moderate oven (180°C, 350°F, Gas Mark 4) for 10–12 minutes. Remove and cool on a wire tray.

HELPFUL HINT
When working with a sticky mixture, it is often easier to achieve the required shapes by using wet hands.

Almond clusters

MAKES 24

3 egg whites
175 g/6 oz castor sugar
225 g/8 oz flaked almonds
few drops of almond essence
Decoration
50 g/2 oz plain chocolate, melted

Whisk the egg whites until stiff then gradually whisk in all the sugar until thick and glossy. This is easier when using an electric mixer on the highest speed. Fold in the almonds and a few drops of almond essence.

Line a baking tray with a sheet of non-stick cooking parchment and place small mounds of the mixture on the tray. Bake in a moderate oven (160°C, 325°F, Gas Mark 3) for 35 minutes then remove and cool on a wire tray.

To decorate the clusters Place the melted chocolate in a small greaseproof piping bag, cut a tiny hole in the point of the bag and pipe swirls of chocolate over the tops of the cakes.

Variation

These little cakes make an ideal base for a dessert. They may be served in individual dishes with scoops of ice cream and topped with a light fruit sauce.

Almond macaroons

MAKES 20–22

2 egg whites
100 g/4 oz castor sugar
100 g/4 oz ground almonds
1 teaspoon ground rice
few drops of almond essence
halved almonds

Whisk the egg whites until stiff. Gradually whisk in the sugar and continue whisking until the mixture is thick and glossy. Stir in the ground almonds, ground rice and a few drops of almond essence.

Place the mixture in a nylon piping bag fitted with a large plain nozzle. Place sheets of rice paper on baking trays and pipe small circles of the mixture on to the paper. Place an almond on top of each macaroon. Bake in a moderate oven (160°C, 325°F, Gas Mark 3) for 15–20 minutes. Carefully remove as much of the rice paper as possible from around the macaroons and cool on a wire tray.

HELPFUL HINT
To pipe out the mixture, hold the bag at a right angle to the baking tray and squeeze gently for the required amount of mixture.

Iced fancies

MAKES APPROXIMATELY 30

1 (23 × 33-cm/9 × 13-inch) Genoese sponge
cake (see page 30)
Icing and decoration
225 g/8 oz glacé icing (see page 114)
food colourings
175 g/6 oz butter icing (see page 112)
various small sweets, cake decorations,
chocolate buttons or vermicelli

Cut the cake into small squares, diamonds and oblong
shapes. A biscuit cutter may be used to cut out rounds
of cake, but this does produce wasted cuttings.

To ice and decorate the fancies The glacé icing may
be coloured in any selection of colours. Divide the
icing into several portions and add a few drops of food
colouring to each. The colour should be delicate.
Cover the cake shapes in glacé icing and leave to set
slightly. Similarly, the butter icing should be delicately
coloured and then placed in a piping bag fitted with a
small star nozzle. The cakes may be decorated with
piped butter icing and various sweets as shown in the
picture. Alternatively, the sides of the cakes can be
spread with butter icing and coated in grated chocolate, chopped nuts, coconut or sugar strands as
preferred. The top of the cakes should be iced with
glacé icing and decorated with piped butter icing.

Coffee butterflies

MAKES 18–20

100 g/4 oz butter or margarine
100 g/4 oz castor sugar
2 eggs
100 g/4 oz self-raising flour
1 tablespoon coffee essence
Icing and decoration
225 g/8 oz coffee butter icing (see page 112)
50 g/2 oz plain chocolate, melted

Cream the butter with the sugar until pale and fluffy.
Gradually beat in the eggs then sieve the flour over the
mixture and fold in gently using a metal spoon. Fold in
the coffee-essence.

Place the mixture in greased bun tins or paper cake
cases placed on a baking tray and bake in a moderate
oven (180°C, 350°F, Gas Mark 4) for 15–20 minutes.
Cool on a wire tray.

To ice and decorate the cakes Slice the tops off of the
cakes and cut them in half to form semi-circles. Place
the butter icing in a piping bag fitted with a small star
nozzle and pipe swirls on top of the cut cakes. Place
the melted chocolate in a greaseproof piping bag, cut a
tiny hole in the point and pipe patterns on each of the
semi-circles. When the chocolate is set, press the
pieces of cake into the swirls of butter icing to form
wings.

HELPFUL HINT
*Use a biscuit cutter to cut
shapes from the cake.
Any excess cake can be
frozen in a sealed plastic
bag to use in recipes that
require cake crumbs,
such as the hedgehog
cake on page 108.*

HELPFUL HINT
*To form the wings, slice
the tops off the cakes and
cut in half. Pipe a small
amount of icing on top of
the cakes and place the
cut pieces at slight angles
in the icing.*

Chapter

SPECIAL OCCASION CAKES

Occasions are always made that much more special when a beautiful cake is served. The following chapter gives recipes for many special occasion cakes from a magnificent three-tier wedding cake to the more simple, yet imaginative Christmas cake

Three-tier wedding cake

1 (30-cm/12-inch) square rich fruit cake (see page 32)
1 (23-cm/9-inch) square rich fruit cake (see page 32)
1 (15-cm/6-inch) square rich fruit cake (see page 32)
Icing and decoration
almond paste (see page 116)
1 (35-cm/14-inch) square silver cake board
1 (25-cm/10-inch) square silver cake board
1 (10-cm/7-inch) square silver cake board
royal icing (see page 117)
primrose coloured piped roses (see page 123)
small silver leaves
silver cake board edging
silver vase
8 cake pillars

Make the cakes, as directed, 2–3 months in advance so that they have time to mature.
To ice and decorate the cakes Cover the cakes with almond paste, as directed, 1–2 weeks before icing, and place the cakes on their appropriate cake boards.

Flat ice the cakes, as directed, until you have completed 4 or 5 layers of icing and have obtained a perfect flat surface. The thinner the layers of icing, the easier it will be to handle.

Make primrose coloured roses, as directed, at least one day before using.

Cut out squares of greaseproof paper the actual size of the iced cakes and fold into quarters. Unfold and fold each edge into the centre to form 16 squares, making a crease along the folded edges. Place the unfolded greaseproof paper on top of each cake and using a pin, prick the four corners on each. Using a greaseproof piping bag fitted with a plain writing nozzle, pipe two straight lines of icing at right angles to each other. Repeat this design. This will then mark the positions for the pillars. Using a finer writing tube, pipe on top of these lines to give a more delicate effect.
To decorate the sides of the cake Cut a strip of greaseproof paper the size of one of the sides of each of the cakes and draw a scalloped edge along each, making five scallops on the large cake, four scallops on the middle sized cake and three on the small cake. Place the paper against the sides of the cakes and prick these designs through using a pin. Using a plain writing nozzle, pipe small dots of icing along the scallops. Position a rose at the top of each scallop with a silver leaf at either side and secure with a little of the icing. Using the same writing nozzle, pipe a beading edge along the bottom edges of each cake. Then using a star shaped nozzle, pipe a shell edge along the top edges. Arrange three roses in the corner of each cake and in the centre of the bottom two tiers.

Using a small palette knife, ice the silver boards with a thin layer of icing and allow to dry hard. Secure the silver paper edging to the boards with a little royal icing.

Place the pillars in position and assemble the cakes at the last minute, placing the vase of flowers on top.

Single-tier wedding cake

1 (23-cm/9-inch) square rich fruit cake (see page 32)
100 g/4 oz crystallised ginger, chopped
100 g/4 oz dried apricots, chopped
2 teaspoons almond essence
Icing and decoration
almond paste (see page 116)
1 (25-cm/10-inch) square silver cake board
royal icing (see page 117)
approximately 50–55 white and apricot coloured piped roses (see page 123)
silver cake board edging
few small pieces of fern

Follow the instructions for making the cake, adding the ginger and apricots with the other dry ingredients and the almond essence with the brandy and orange juice. Make the cake 2–3 months in advance so it has time to mature.

To ice and decorate the cake Cover the cake with almond paste 1–2 weeks before icing and place on the cake board. Flat ice the cake, as directed, until you have completed four to five layers of icing and a perfectly flat surface is attained.

Make the roses at least one day before using. Arrange a cluster of roses on each of the corners of the cake, trailing one or two small roses down the sides. Decide which roses to use before securing them to the cake with a little icing. Using a small palette knife, ice the silver board with a thin layer of icing. Allow to dry hard. Use a greaseproof piping bag fitted with a small star shaped nozzle to pipe the edge on the top and bottom of the cake. Arrange a few tiny roses on the side of each cake and three larger ones in the middle of the cake. Secure the board edging with a little icing. Place the fern on the cake at the last minute.

Variation

Substitute fondant icing (see page 115) for the flat royal icing. Use double the quantity given in the recipe. Colour and use the leftover to make moulded roses (see page 123) for the decoration. Make up a small quantity of royal icing to pipe the top and bottom edgings.

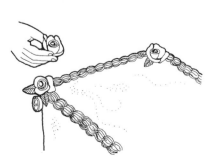

HELPFUL HINT
It may be easier to arrange the piped roses on the cake prior to the wedding reception as they may become damaged during transit.

Pink christening cake

1 (20-cm/8-inch) round rich fruit cake (see
page 32)
Icing and decoration
almond paste (see page 116)
1 (25-cm/10-inch) round silver cake board
royal icing (see page 117)
pink food colouring

Make the cake, as directed, 2–3 months in advance so
that it has time to mature.

To ice and decorate the cake Cover the cake with
almond paste, as directed, 1–2 weeks before icing and
place on the silver cake board.

Make up the icing and reserve a little of the white
icing for piping. Colour the remainder pink. Flat ice the
cake as directed, using the pink icing. Using a small
palette knife, cover the silver board with a thin layer of
icing and allow to dry hard.

Cut a strip of greaseproof paper the circumference
and width of the sides of the cake and draw a scalloped
edge, evenly all the way round. Place around the cake
and secure with a pin and then prick through the
design on to the cake. Remove the greaseproof paper
and using a greaseproof piping bag fitted with a writing
nozzle, pipe small dots along the scallops with the
white icing, and vertical dots in between each scallop.
Using the same nozzle, pipe the trellis along the bottom
edge of the cake. Pipe a series of parallel lines at an
angle all round the cake. Then pipe another layer of
parallel lines over the top in the opposite direction.
Repeat this twice, extending the length of the lines
slightly over each layer. Pipe a line of small dots either
side of the trellis. Using the same writing nozzle, pipe
the name of the child to be christened. Pipe a row of
stars, using a star shaped nozzle along the top edge.

Silver wedding cake

1 (20-cm/8-inch) square rich fruit cake (see
page 32)
Icing and decoration
almond paste (see page 116)
1 (23-cm/9-inch) square silver cake board
royal icing (see page 117)
crystallised flowers (see page 122)
silver cake decorations (optional)
silver cake board edging

Make the cake, as directed, 2–3 months in advance
so that it has time to mature.

To ice and decorate the cake Cover the cake with
almond paste, as directed, 1–2 weeks before icing and
place on a silver cake board.

Make up the icing and flat ice the cake, as directed.
Decorate with crystallised flowers and silver cake
decorations, if liked. Place the silver board edging
around the sides of the cake, securing with a little icing.
Pipe a shell border on the top and bottom edges of the
cake.

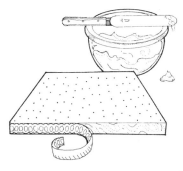

HELPFUL HINT
*To secure the cake board
edging, using a small
palette knife, spread a
thin layer of icing around
the edge of the board.
Before it dries, press on
the edging.*

69

Ski cake

1 (18-cm/7-inch) square rich fruit cake
(see page 32)
almond paste (see page 116)
1 (20-cm/8-inch) square silver cake board
royal icing (see page 117)
runouts (see page 122)
ribbon

Make the cake, as directed, 2–3 months in advance so that it has time to mature.

To ice and decorate the cake Cover the cake with the almond paste, as directed, 1–2 weeks before icing and place on a silver cake board.

Make up the icing and flat ice the cake, as directed, reserving a little for piping. Make the mouse runouts as shown, or design a runout of your own and place on top of the cake, securing with a little icing. Using a greaseproof piping bag fitted with a star shaped nozzle, decorate the top and bottom edges of the cake with the reserved icing. Tie a ribbon around the cake.

Fondant-iced Christmas cake

1 (18-cm/7-inch) round rich fruit cake (see page 32)
Icing and decoration
almond paste (see page 116)
1 (20-cm/8-inch) round silver cake board
fondant icing (see page 115)
red and green food colouring
candle
ribbon

Make the cake, as directed, 2–3 months in advance so that it has time to mature.

To ice and decorate the cake Cover the cake with almond paste, as directed, 1–2 weeks before icing and place on a silver cake board.

Make up the fondant icing, as directed, reserving trimmings and cover the cake. Allow to dry overnight before decorating.

Using the trimmings of the fondant icing, colour a little green and some red and mould to resemble holly. Arrange the holly in a circle on top of the cake and secure a candle in the centre. Tie a ribbon around the edge of the cake.

Snow-peaked cake

1 (15-cm/6-inch) round rich fruit cake (see page 32)
Icing and decoration
almond paste (see page 116)
1 (18-cm/7-inch) round silver cake board
royal icing (see page 117)
Christmas cake decorations
ribbon

Make the cake, as directed, 2–3 months in advance so that it has time to mature.

To ice and decorate the cake Cover the cake with almond paste, as directed, 1–2 weeks before icing and place on the silver cake board. Make up the icing, as directed, and flat ice the sides. When you have completed two or three layers of icing on the sides, rough ice the top. To rough ice, cover the top completely with icing and smooth evenly, then using the tip of a palette knife, dip it into the icing and press the tip of the knife on to the surface of the icing and draw away to form a peak. Repeat this process until the top of the cake is covered in peaks of icing. Decorate with Christmas decorations, and tie a ribbon around the cake.

Chocolate snowman

175 g/6 oz butter or margarine
175 g/6 oz castor sugar
3 eggs
175 g/6 oz self-raising flour
2 tablespoons cocoa powder
1 teaspoon baking powder
Icing and decoration
50 g/2 oz apricot jam
350 g/12 oz American frosting (see page 115)
few Smarties
paper hat (optional)

Place the butter, sugar and eggs in a bowl. Sieve the flour, cocoa powder and baking powder over the butter mixture and beat all the ingredients together thoroughly until pale chocolate in colour and of a soft dropping consistency. Grease one 300-ml/½-pint basin and one 900-ml/1½-pint basin thoroughly. Divide the mixture between the two basins and bake in a moderate oven (160°C, 325°F, Gas Mark 3) for 1 hour 20 minutes for the small cake and 1 hour 25 minutes for the larger cake. Turn out and cool on a wire tray.
To ice and decorate the cake Trim the smaller cake around the wider edge to round it off slightly so that it will sit securely on the base. Spread the jam on top of the larger cake and place the small cake on top. Cover the cake completely in frosting. Place chocolate Smarties on the head to form eyes and halved red Smarties to form a mouth and nose. Place a few Smarties on the body to represent buttons. The snowman may have a paper hat on his head.

Father Christmas

2 basin cakes (see chocolate snowman, page 72)
50 g/2 oz apricot jam
Icing and decoration
350 g/12 oz fondant icing (see page 115)
red food colouring
icing sugar
two chocolate drops
piece of liquorice
liquorice allsorts
small paper bag or one made out of a scrap of
material (optional)

Make the basin cakes as for the chocolate snowman but omitting the cocoa powder. Trim and assemble the cakes as for the snowman.
To ice and decorate the cake Colour two thirds of the icing a good strong red. Cut the remaining icing in half and colour one piece pale pink. Leave the remaining icing white.

Divide the red icing into three pieces. Use one piece, rolled out on a board dusted with icing sugar, to cover the front of the main cake. Place the piece of liquorice across the cake to form a belt and a liquorice sweet as a buckle. Roll out the second piece of red icing and drape over the back of the cake to complete the cloak. Roll out the pink icing and cover the front of the head with it. Deepen the colour in the cheeks using a small paint brush and diluted food colouring. Mould the remaining red icing around the head for the hat, reserving a small piece for the nose. Use the white icing to shape the remaining features, the hair, beard and the border of the cloak. Use chocolate drops for the eyes. Place the liquorice allsorts in the bag and arrange next to Father Christmas, if liked.

HELPFUL HINT
To trim the cake, place it on a board wider end down and with a sharp pointed knife, cut downwards around the bottom of the cake on to the board.

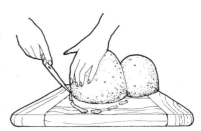

HELPFUL HINT
Place the pudding basins on a baking tray for easy removal from the oven.

Christmas tree

1 (23 × 33-cm/9 × 13-inch) sandwich cake (see
boat cake page 103)
Icing and decoration
225 g/8 oz butter icing (see page 112)
green food colouring
2 teaspoons cocoa powder
2 teaspoons boiling water
mini chocolate roll
candles
liquorice allsorts
small star
small piece ribbon

Cut out a piece of greaseproof paper to the same size
as the cake. Draw the shape of the Christmas tree on
the paper and use as a template to cut out the cake
(see helpful hint). Cut out the tub for the tree from the
spare pieces of cake.
To ice and decorate the cake Reserve one tablespoon of butter icing. Colour the remaining icing green
and use to cover the cake completely. Fork the icing to
give a branch effect. Cream the cocoa powder with the
boiling water. Cool and mix with the remaining butter
icing. Use the chocolate icing to cover the tub. Place
the chocolate roll at the base of the tree as the trunk
and put the tub in position. Decorate with candles,
sweets, a star and a ribbon.

Parcel cakes

1 (23 × 33-cm/9 × 13-inch) sandwich cake (see
boat cake, page 103)
Icing and decoration
350 g/12 oz butter icing (see page 112)
various food colourings
chocolate vermicelli
tinted dragees
silver balls

Cut the cake into small square or oblong shapes.
To ice and decorate the cakes Divide the butter icing
into small portions and colour with various food
colourings. Cover each square completely in butter
icing and press chocolate vermicelli around some of
the cakes using a palette knife. Using a greaseproof
piping bag fitted with a ribbon nozzle, pipe the ribbons
on the cakes. Decorate with tinted dragees or silver
balls.

Variation
Instead of using butter icing to cover the cakes, they
may be covered with thinly rolled out almond paste
(see page 116). Brush the squares of cake with
warmed apricot jam to make the almond paste stick.
Decorate as liked with shapes moulded from almond
paste.

HELPFUL HINT
*Cut a Christmas tree
shape from paper and
face it on the baked cake.
Cut around the shape to
make the tree. Left over
pieces of cake may be
frozen for future use or
used in a trifle.*

HELPFUL HINT
*To tint icings, dip a metal
skewer into the bottle of
food colouring and shake
the drops from the
skewer into the icing. This
method ensures that the
icing does not become
too brightly coloured.*

Valentine's cake

225 g/8 oz butter or margarine
225 g/8 oz castor sugar
grated rind of 2 lemons
4 eggs
225 g/8 oz self-raising flour
Icing and decoration
375 g/12 oz lemon butter icing (see page 112)
yellow food colouring
fresh flowers
angelica leaves
small pieces of fern (optional)

Cream the butter with the castor sugar and lemon rind until pale and fluffy. Gradually beat in the eggs. Sieve the flour over the creamed mixture and fold in carefully using a metal spoon.

Grease three heart-shaped tins measuring 23 cm/ 9 inches, 18 cm/7 inches and 12 cm/4¾ inches from the point to the top of the heart. Divided the mixture proportionally between the three tins and bake in a moderate oven (160°C, 325°F, Gas Mark 3) for 30–40 minutes. Turn out and cool on a wire tray.

To ice and decorate the cakes Cover the top of each cake thinly with some of the butter icing. On a suitable cake board or plate, place all three cakes on top of each other with the larger cake on the bottom. Colour the remaining icing a delicate yellow and use some to cover the cake completely. Place the remaining butter icing in a greaseproof piping bag fitted with a small star shaped nozzle and pipe an edging on the cake. Arrange fresh flowers on the cake together with angelica leaves and fern, if liked.

Mother's Day cake

175 g/6 oz butter or margarine
175 g/6 oz castor sugar
3 eggs
100 g/4 oz glacé cherries
50 g/2 oz crystallised ginger, chopped
50 g/2 oz crystallised pineapple, chopped
50 g/2 oz citron peel, chopped
225 g/8 oz self-raising flour
Icing and decoration
225 g/8 oz glacé icing (see page 114)
50 g/2 oz glacé cherries
2 tablespoons castor sugar
few pieces of angelica

Cream the butter with the sugar until pale and fluffy. Gradually beat in the eggs. Wash, drain and chop the cherries. Add to the other chopped ingredients and coat thoroughly in 2 tablespoons of the measured flour.

Sieve the flour over the creamed mixture and fold in gently using a metal spoon. Gently fold in the chopped ingredients. Transfer the mixture to a lined and greased 20-cm/8-inch cake tin, smooth over the surface slightly and bake in a moderate oven (160°C, 325°F, Gas Mark 3) for 1¼ hours. Turn out and cool on a wire tray.

To ice and decorate the cake Pour the glacé icing over the cake, allowing it to drizzle down the sides. Coat the glacé cherries in the castor sugar and place small pieces of angelica in the top of them to form stalks. Arrange the cherries on top of the cake.

Easter Chick

2 basin cakes (see chocolate snowman,
page 72)
Icing and decoration
225 g/8 oz butter icing (see page 112)
few drops of yellow food colouring
chocolate drops
50 g/2 oz almond paste, made-up weight
(see page 116)*
red ribbon
Easter bonnet made from coloured paper
and fresh flowers (optional)

**If preferred, you can use ready prepared almond paste
available from most supermarkets.*

Make the cakes as for the chocolate snowman but
omitting the cocoa powder.
To ice and decorate the cakes Colour the butter icing
with the yellow food colouring. Spread a little icing on
top of the larger cake and place the smaller cake on
top. Trim the edges of the smaller cake to form the
neck of the chick. Cover the cakes completely with the
icing and rough it up for a feather effect using a fork.
Place chocolate drops on the cake to form eyes and
shape one third of the almond paste to form a beak.
Tie a bow around the neck and shape the remaining
almond paste for the feet. Place an Easter bonnet with
fresh flowers on top of the cake, if liked.

Simnel cake

175 g/6 oz butter or margarine
175 g/6 oz dark soft brown sugar
3 eggs
225 g/8 oz self-raising flour
1 teaspoon mixed spice
350 g/12 oz sultanas
100 g/4 oz mixed chopped peel
225 g/8 oz raisins
50 g/2 oz almonds, chopped
4–5 tablespoons milk
Icing and decoration
675 g/1½ lb almond paste (see page 116)
sieved apricot jam
little glacé icing (see page 114)

Place all the cake ingredients in a mixing bowl and
beat with a wooden spoon until well mixed. Place half
the mixture in a prepared 20-cm/8-inch cake tin.
Roll out 225 g/8 oz of the almond paste into a circle
measuring 20 cm/8 inches in diameter. Place the paste
on top of the cake mixture and then spoon the
remaining mixture over it, smoothing the surface
evenly. Protect the outside of the tin with newspaper.
Bake in a moderate oven (160°C, 325°F, Gas Mark 3)
for 2 hours, then reduce the temperature to a cool
oven (150°C, 300°F, Gas Mark 2) for a further 50–60
minutes. Allow to cool and turn out on to a wire tray.
To ice and decorate the cake Roll out 225 g/8 oz of
the almond paste into a round to fit the top of the cake.
Brush the top of the cake with apricot jam and secure
the almond paste on top. Use a fork to serrate the
edge. Divide the remaining almond paste into 11 equal
sized pieces and roll into balls. Arrange them around
the top edge of the cake, securing each with a little
jam. Using a fork, press each ball firmly so that they
flatten. Brush with a little beaten egg white and place
under a hot grill until lightly browned.
Pour the glacé icing into the centre.

Evil witches

MAKES 12

orange cake mixture made with 100 g/4 oz butter
etc. (see Bonfire cake, opposite)
Icing and decoration
225 g/8 oz plain chocolate, melted
225 g/8 oz almond paste, made-up weight (see page
116)*
red food colouring
stiff black paper

**If preferred, you can use ready prepared almond paste
available from most supermarkets.*

Divide the cake mixture between twelve greased
dariole moulds and bake in a moderate oven (180°C,
350°F, Gas Mark 4) for 25–30 minutes. Turn out and
cool on a wire tray.

To ice and decorate the cakes Cover the cakes
completely in melted chocolate. Knead the almond
paste with a few drops of red food colouring to give a
good red colour. Use tiny pieces of almond paste to
make the facial features and place these on the
witches. Roll out the remaining almond paste and cut
semi-circles out of it to wrap around the back of the
witches to form cloaks.

The hats are made out of stiff black paper. Turn one
of the dariole moulds upside down on a piece of
paper. Draw a circle around the tin to form the brim of
the hat. Cut out a triangle of paper measuring
approximately 14 cm/5½ inches along the largest sides.
Form the triangle into a cone shape, secure with sticky
tape and trim the edges. Place the cone in the middle
of the circle of paper and secure, on the inside of the
cone, with sticky tape. Place the hats on top of the
cakes.

Bonfire cake

100 g/4 oz butter or margarine
100 g/4 oz castor sugar
grated rind of 2 oranges
2 eggs
100 g/4 oz self-raising flour
1 tablespoon orange juice
Icing and decoration
225 g/8 oz orange butter icing (see page 112)
orange and red food colouring
orange-flavoured chocolate sticks
pared orange rind

Cream the butter with the sugar and orange rind until pale and fluffy. Gradually beat in the eggs. Sieve the flour over the mixture and fold in gently using a metal spoon. Finally, fold in the orange juice. Turn into a well greased 900-ml/1½-pint pudding basin and bake in a moderate oven (160°C, 325°F, Gas Mark 3) for 1 hour 25 minutes or until well risen, golden in colour and firm to the touch. Turn out and cool on a wire tray.

To ice and decorate the cake Colour the butter icing orange and use to cover the cake completely, forking it into peaks. Dilute a little red food colouring with water and, using a fine paint brush, tinge the peaks of butter icing slightly red. Arrange the chocolate sticks over the cake and top with pieces of pared orange rind to represent flames.

Chocolate piggy cake

1 (18-cm/7-inch) Victoria sandwich (see page 20)
Filling and icing
3 tablespoons raspberry jam
225 g/8 oz butter icing (see page 112)
pink or blue food colouring
1 tablespoon cocoa powder
boiling water
225 g/8 oz almond paste, made-up weight (see page 116)*
candles

If preferred, you can use ready prepared almond paste available from most supermarkets.

To fill and ice the cake Sandwich the cake layers together with the raspberry jam. Colour the butter icing a pale shade of either pink or blue. Mix the cocoa powder to a cream with a little boiling water. Knead the almond paste until pliable, then gradually knead in the creamed cocoa powder. Roll out on to a surface sieved with icing sugar. Using a pig shaped biscuit cutter, cut out eight pigs from the almond paste.

Cover the top and sides of the cake with some icing. Mark the top of the cake with a round bladed knife and the sides with a serrated scraper. Using a greaseproof piping bag fitted with a star shaped nozzle, pipe the edging on the cake. Arrange the chocolate pigs around the side of the cake and the candles on top.

Granny cake

175 g/6 oz butter or margarine
175 g/6 oz castor sugar
grated rind of 2 oranges
3 eggs
250 g/9 oz self-raising flour
1½ teaspoons baking powder
Filling and icing
50 g/2 oz butter
75 g/3 oz icing sugar, sieved
grated rind of 1 large orange
100 g/4 oz ground almonds
4 tablespoons orange juice
225 g/8 oz almond paste (see page 116)
2–3 tablespoons apricot jam, warmed and sieved
350 g/12 oz fondant icing (see page 115)
red and yellow food colouring
icing sugar
ribbon
moulded flowers and leaves (see page 123)

Place all the cake ingredients in a bowl and beat together, until smooth. Transfer the mixture to a bottom-lined and greased 20-cm/8-inch cake tin. Bake at (180°C, 350°F, Gas Mark 4) for 1–1¼ hours.

To fill and ice the cake Cream the butter with the icing sugar and orange rind until pale and fluffy. Gradually beat in the ground almonds and juice.

Cut through the cake horizontally and sandwich the layers together with the cream. Cover the cake with almond paste as directed. Leave to dry out overnight.

Carefully colour the fondant icing by kneading in drops of the food colouring. Roll out on a surface sieved with icing sugar to give a round of approximately 36 cm/14 inches diameter. Brush the cake with a little apricot jam. Carefully lift the fondant over the cake and smooth it down evenly using fingertips dipped in sieved icing sugar or cornflour and trim. Leave to dry, then finish as shown.

Individual birthday cake

50 g/2 oz butter or margarine
50 g/2 oz castor sugar
few drops of vanilla essence
1 egg
75 g/3 oz self-raising flour
Icing and decoration
1 gold doily
piece of ribbon
50 g/2 oz icing sugar, sieved
2 teaspoons water
slice of citron peel

Cream the butter with the sugar and vanilla essence until pale and fluffy. Gradually beat in the egg then sieve the flour over the mixture and fold in gently using a metal spoon.

Line and grease a 9-cm/3½-inch tin, measuring approximately 10 cm/4 inches in depth. Place the mixture in the tin, smooth the surface and bake in a moderate oven (160°C, 325°F, Gas Mark 3) for 50–60 minutes. Turn out and cool on a wire tray.

To ice and decorate the cake Fold a doily around the cake and tie a bow of ribbon around it. Mix the icing sugar with the water to give a thick glacé icing. Place the icing on top of the cake and decorate with a slice of citron peel.

HELPFUL HINT
To ensure that a white glacé icing does not become grey, sieve the icing sugar through a nylon (not metal) sieve.

18th birthday cake

1 (23-cm/9-inch) round rich fruit cake (see page 32)
Icing and decoration
almond paste (see page 116)
1 (25-cm/10-inch) round silver cake board
royal icing (see page 117)
blue food colouring
silver key

Make the cake, as directed, 2–3 months in advance, so that it has time to mature.

To ice and decorate the cake Cover the cake with almond paste, as directed, 1–2 weeks before icing and place on the silver cake board.

Make up the icing as directed and reserve a little of the white icing for piping. Colour the remainder blue. Flat ice the cake with the blue icing as shown using a serrated scraper on the sides of the cake, to give a ridged effect. Using a palette knife, cover the silver board with a thin layer of icing.

Using a greaseproof piping bag fitted with a star shape nozzle, pipe a shell border with the white icing around the top and bottom edges of the cake. Then using a writing nozzle, pipe **congratulations** on top of the cake. Pipe three parallel lines across the top of the cake. When these are dry pipe another line on top of each to give a bolder design. Decorate with a silver key.

HELPFUL HINT
When writing with icing, have the royal icing on the soft side so that it flows smoothly and freely from the nozzle. Hold the nozzle about 2.5 cm/1 inch from the surface of the cake.

Chapter

GATEAUX

The mouth-watering gâteaux in this chapter may at first glance daunt you, but by following the clearly explained recipes and using the colour pictures as your guide, you'll be able to achieve success and impress your family and guests. The helpful hints and drawings will guide you through the less easy stages. These gâteaux may be served as a dessert or made for afternoon tea — the peach gâteau makes a particularly delightful summer dessert.

Hazelnut cream bombe

100 g/4 oz hazelnuts, finely chopped
3 eggs
175 g/6 oz castor sugar
150 g/5 oz plain flour
grated rind of 2 oranges
Filling and decoration
300 ml/½ pint double cream
2 tablespoons orange juice
2 tablespoons Cointreau
1 orange
50 g/2 oz hazelnuts

Lightly toast the hazelnuts. Whisk the eggs with the sugar until pale and thick. Sift the flour over the mixture and carefully fold in together with the hazelnuts and orange rind.

Turn into a well greased 1.15-litre/2-pint pudding basin and bake in a moderate oven (180°C, 350°F, Gas Mark 4) for 45–50 minutes. Turn out and cool on a wire tray.

Whip the cream with the orange juice and Cointreau until thick. Cut the cake into three, horizontally, and sandwich together with some of the cream. Reserve a third of the cream for piping and use the remainder to completely cover the bombe.

Decorate with pared orange rind, orange slices, piped cream and hazelnuts.

Mocha roulade

3 teaspoons instant coffee powder
1 tablespoon hot water
100 g/4 oz plain chocolate
4 eggs, separated
100 g/4 oz castor sugar
Decoration
300 ml/½ pint double cream
little sifted icing sugar
chocolate shapes (see page 120)

Blend the coffee with the hot water, add the chocolate and melt in a basin over a saucepan of hot water. Allow to cool. Whisk the egg yolks and sugar until thick. Carefully fold in the melted chocolate. Whisk the egg whites until stiff then fold into the mixture. Pour into a lined and greased 33- x 23-cm/13- x 9-inch Swiss roll tin and bake in a moderate oven (180°C, 350°F, Gas Mark 4) for 15–20 minutes. Immediately after taking the cake out of the oven cover it (in the tin) with a damp teatowel and leave covered overnight.

To decorate the roulade Carefully turn the cake out on to sugared paper, remove the lining paper. Whip the cream and spread over the cake, reserving a little for piping. Roll up like a Swiss roll and dust with sifted icing sugar. Pipe down the centre of the roll with the reserved cream and decorate with chocolate shapes.

Spicy pear surprise

100 g/4 oz butter or margarine
100 g/4 oz castor sugar
½ teaspoon cinnamon, preferably freshly ground
grated rind of 1 orange
2 eggs
100 g/4 oz self-raising flour
Filling and decoration
300 ml/½ pint double cream
2 tablespoons rum
1 tablespoon castor sugar
1 (411-g/14½-oz) can pear halves
1 orange, thinly sliced and quartered

Cream the butter with the sugar, cinnamon and orange rind until pale and fluffy. Gradually beat in the eggs then sieve the flour over the mixture and fold in gently using a metal spoon. Grease one 20-cm/8-inch sponge flan tin; bottom-line and grease one 20-cm/8-inch sandwich tin. Divide the mixture between the two tins, allowing slightly more for the sandwich tin, and spread out evenly. Bake in a moderate oven (160°C, 325°F, Gas Mark 3) for 35–40 minutes. Turn out and cool on a wire tray.
To fill and decorate the cake Whip the cream with the rum and sugar until thick. Drain the pears thoroughly and arrange in the flan. Spread some of the cream over them and place the sandwich cake on top. Spread half of the remaining cream over the top of the cake. Using a large star nozzle, pipe a cream edging around the top of the cake. Decorate with quartered orange slices.

Variation
Fresh pears are delicious in this gâteau. They should be peeled, cored and halved then poached gently in a little syrup until just soft before using to fill the flan.

Tipsy ring

100 g/4 oz butter or margarine
100 g/4 oz castor sugar
2 tablespoons ginger wine
2 eggs
100 g/4 oz self-raising flour
25 g/1 oz cocoa powder
3 tablespoons ginger wine
Icing and decoration
175 g/6 oz plain chocolate
50 g/2 oz butter
150 ml/¼ pint double cream
few pieces of crystallised ginger

Cream the butter with the sugar and ginger wine until pale and fluffy. Gradually beat in the eggs. Sieve the flour with the cocoa powder and fold into the creamed mixture using a metal spoon. Turn into a well greased 23-cm/9-inch ring tin and bake in a moderate oven (160°C, 325°F, Gas Mark 3) for 40–50 minutes. Turn out and cool on a wire tray. Whilst the cake is still warm, drizzle the ginger wine over it, until absorbed.
To ice and decorate the ring Melt the chocolate with the butter. Allow to cool slightly then drizzle over the cake. Whip the cream until stiff and, using a nylon piping bag fitted with a large star nozzle, pipe the cream along the top of the cake. Decorate with pieces of crystallised ginger.

Variation
Use 1 tablespoon of coffee essence instead of the cocoa powder and rum instead of the ginger wine. Soak the cake in rum instead of ginger wine and ice and decorate the cake as above.

84

Black Forest gâteau

3 eggs
125 g/4 oz castor sugar
75 g/3 oz plain flour
15 g/½ oz cocoa powder
Filling
1 (425-g/15-oz) can pitted black cherries
1 tablespoon arrowroot
Kirsch
300 ml/½ pint double cream
grated chocolate to decorate

Place the eggs and sugar in a basin and whisk over a saucepan of hot water until thick and pale in colour. Remove from the heat and continue to whisk until cool. Sieve the flour and cocoa powder together and gently fold into the mixture, using a metal spoon. Pour into a bottom-lined and greased 20-cm/8-inch cake tin. Bake in a moderately hot oven (190°C, 375°F, Gas Mark 5) for 35–40 minutes. Turn out and cool on a wire tray.

To fill and decorate the gâteau Drain the juice from the cherries and blend a little with the arrowroot. Bring the remainder of the juice to the boil, then pour on to the blended arrowroot and return to the heat to thicken, stirring continuously. Add the cherries to the syrup and allow to cool.

Cut the cake in half and sprinkle the base with a little Kirsch. Whip the cream and with a nylon piping bag fitted with a large star nozzle pipe a circle of cream around the outside edge of the base. Fill the centre with half of the cherry mixture. Sprinkle the second layer of cake with a little Kirsch and place on top of the filling. Spread a little cream around the edge of the gâteau and press grated chocolate on top using a palette knife. Pipe swirls of cream on top of the gâteau and fill the centre with the remaining cherries. Sprinkle a little grated chocolate on the swirls of cream.

Austrian coffee gâteau

125 g/4 oz butter or margarine
125 g/4 oz castor sugar
2 eggs
125 g/4 oz self-raising flour
2 tablespoons coffee essence
grated rind of 1 lemon
Syrup
150 ml/¼ pint black coffee
50 g/2 oz castor sugar
1 tablespoon brandy
Decoration
300 ml/½ pint double cream
chocolate curls (see page 120)

Cream the butter and sugar together until light and fluffy. Add the eggs one at a time, adding a little of the flour with the second egg. Beat in the coffee essence, then fold in the remaining flour with the grated lemon rind. Place in a greased 20-cm/8-inch ring tin and bake in a moderate oven (160°C, 325°F, Gas mark 3) for 40–50 minutes. Turn out and cool on a wire tray.

To make the syrup Heat the coffee and sugar together in a saucepan until the sugar is dissolved, then add the brandy and simmer for 5 minutes. Allow to cool. Prick the cake with a skewer and pour over the syrup, a little at a time, until it is all absorbed.

To decorate the gâteau Whip the cream and spread a little all over the cake. Using a nylon piping bag, pipe the remainder around the edge and decorate with the chocolate curls.

HELPFUL HINT
Place the cake on a wire tray with a large plate underneath to catch the syrup. This can be saved and poured over the cake again until all is absorbed.

Honey hazelnut gâteau

3 eggs
175 g/6 oz clear honey
100 g/4 oz hazelnuts, chopped
100 g/4 oz plain flour
Filling and decoration
450 ml/¾ pint double cream
4 tablespoons clear honey
100 g/4 oz hazelnuts, chopped
50 g/2 oz whole hazelnuts

Whisk the eggs with the honey until pale and thick. Meanwhile, lightly toast the chopped hazelnuts until pale golden in colour. Sieve the flour and mix with the hazelnuts then fold lightly into the whisked mixture. Turn into a lined and greased 23- x 33-cm/9- x 13-inch Swiss roll tin and bake in a moderately hot oven (200°C, 400°F, Gas Mark 6) for 10–15 minutes. Turn out on to a wire tray, remove the greaseproof paper and leave to cool.

Whip the cream with the honey. Lightly toast the chopped hazelnuts. Cut the cake into three oblong pieces and sandwich together with half the cream. Spread the sides of the gâteau with cream and press the chopped hazelnuts on them. Using a small star nozzle, pipe around the edge of the cake. Mix the whole hazelnuts with the honey, warming it slightly if necessary, and carefully spoon over the top of the cake. Serve immediately.

Minted lemon gâteau

125 g/4 oz castor sugar
3 eggs
75 g/3 oz plain flour
40 g/1½ oz butter or margarine, melted
few sprigs of mint, finely chopped
grated rind of 1 lemon
Decoration
300 ml/½ pint double cream
fresh lemon slices
few sprigs of crystallised mint (see page 122)

Whisk the sugar and eggs together in a basin over a saucepan of hot water until mixture is thick and pale in colour. Sieve the flour twice and fold into the whisked mixture with the chopped mint and lemon rind. Place in a greased and floured 20-cm/8-inch ring tin. Bake in a moderately hot oven (190°C, 375°F, Gas Mark 5) for 20 minutes. Turn out very carefully and cool on a wire tray.

To decorate the gâteau Whip the cream and spread a little all over the gâteau. Pipe a border of cream around the top edge and decorate the edge with halved fresh lemon slices and sprigs of crystallised mint.

HELPFUL HINT
An easy way of warming honey is to stand the pot in a saucepan of hot water for a few minutes before using it.

HELPFUL HINT
Sprinkle a little castor sugar on to the mint to make it easier to chop. Use a pastry brush to remove all the grated rind from the grater.

Tropical gâteau

2 eggs
75 g/3 oz castor sugar
75 g/3 oz plain flour
2 tablespoons rum
Filling and decoration
1 small fresh pineapple
225 g/8 oz fresh dates
2 tablespoons rum
1 tablespoon soft brown sugar
300 ml/½ pint double cream
100 g/4 oz long thread coconut, lightly toasted
angelica leaves

Whisk the eggs with the sugar until pale and thick. Sieve the flour over the eggs and sprinkle over the rum. Fold in carefully using a metal spoon.

Bottom-line and grease a Swiss roll tin measuring 18 × 28 cm/7 × 11 inches. Turn the mixture into the tin and spread out evenly. Bake in a moderate oven (160°C, 325°F, Gas Mark 3) for 30–35 minutes. Turn out and cool on a wire tray, removing the greaseproof paper while the cake is still hot.

To fill and decorate the gâteau Slice and peel the pineapple then cut into neat pieces. Reserve approximately one third of the pineapple for decoration. Stone and chop the dates. Mix the pineapple, dates and rum together. Sprinkle over the sugar and leave for at least 1 hour.

Slice the cake lengthways into two long, narrow, oblong pieces. Drain the juices off the fruit and sprinkle the juice over the pieces of cake. Arrange the fruit on one piece of cake and place the second piece on top. Whip the cream until stiff. Cover the sides and top of the cake thinly with cream and press the coconut against the sides of the cake using a palette knife. Place the remaining cream in a nylon piping bag fitted with a large star nozzle and pipe a line of cream down the middle of the cake. Arrange the reserved pineapple on either side of the cream and decorate with angelica leaves.

Creamy peach meringue

3 egg whites
175 g/6 oz castor sugar
50 g/2 oz plain chocolate, finely grated
Filling and decoration
3 large peaches
lemon juice
300 ml/½ pint double cream
chocolate curls (see page 120)

Whisk the egg whites until stiff. Sprinkle over the castor sugar and whisk in vigorously until thick and glossy. Gently fold in the grated chocolate using a metal spoon.

Bottom-line two 20-cm/8-inch sandwich tins with non-stick baking parchment. Grease thoroughly. Divide the mixture between the two tins and smooth the top. Bake in a moderately hot oven (180°C, 350°F, Gas Mark 4) for 40–45 minutes. Allow to cool completely in the tins.

To ice and decorate the meringue Halve and stone the peaches. Remove the skin from one and a half peaches. Slice all the peaches thinly and sprinkle with a little lemon juice to prevent discoloration. Whip the cream until stiff.

Carefully remove the baking parchment from the base of the cakes. Place one layer on the serving dish and spread half the cream over it. Arrange the peeled peach slices on top and sandwich with the remaining layer of cake. Spread the remaining cream on top and arrange the unpeeled peach slices on the cake. Decorate with chocolate curls.

HELPFUL HINT
If preferred, you could use 150 ml/¼ pint double cream and 150 ml/¼ pint whipping cream. This mixture will still whip and hold its shape and will be a little less expensive.

HELPFUL HINT
To remove the skin from fresh peaches, place them in a bowl of boiling water for about 30 seconds. Lift out and peel away the skins.

Loganberry gâteau

4 eggs
125 g/4 oz castor sugar
grated rind of ½ lemon
75 g/3 oz plain flour
25 g/1 oz cornflour
25 g/1 oz butter, melted
Filling and decoration
450 g/1 lb loganberries
6 tablespoons sherry
450 ml/¾ pint double cream, whipped
finely grated chocolate

Place the eggs, sugar and lemon rind in a basin and whisk over a saucepan of hot water until pale and thick. Remove from the heat and continue to whisk until cool. Fold in the sieved flour and cornflour, and the melted butter, using a metal spoon. Pour into a bottom-lined and greased 20-cm/8-inch square cake tin and bake in a moderately hot oven (190°C, 375°F, Gas Mark 5) for 30–35 minutes. Turn out and cool on a wire tray.

To fill and decorate the gâteau Reserve half the loganberries for decoration. Cut the cake into three, horizontally. Sprinkle the bottom layer with a little of the sherry and spread with some whipped cream, and a portion of the loganberries. Repeat with the second sponge layer on top. Top with the remaining sponge layer, cover the sides with a thin layer of cream and press the grated chocolate all over the sides with a palette knife. Cover the top with a thin layer of cream and, using a nylon piping bag, pipe a border of cream around the edges. Fill with the remaining loganberries and decorate with loganberry or raspberry leaves if available.

Autumn gâteau

175 g/6 oz butter or margarine
175 g/6 oz castor sugar
3 eggs
2 medium cooking apples, peeled, cored
and grated
200 g/7 oz self-raising flour
75 g/3 oz desiccated coconut
Filling and decoration
2 tablespoons cornflour
2 tablespoons clear honey
250 ml/8 fl oz apple juice
1 large red dessert apple
juice of ½ lemon
300 ml/½ pint double cream
shredded coconut

Cream the butter with the sugar until pale and fluffy. Gradually beat in the eggs and stir in the grated apples. Sieve the flour over the mixture and fold in gently together with the coconut. Turn into a bottom-lined and greased 18-cm/7-inch square cake tin and bake in a moderate oven (160°C, 325°F, Gas Mark 3) for 1¾ hours. Turn out and cool on a wire tray.

To fill and decorate the gâteau Blend the cornflour with the honey and a little of the apple juice until smooth. Heat the remaining juice until very warm then stir into the blended cornflour. Return the mixture to the saucepan, bring to the boil, stirring continuously and cook for 3–4 minutes. Cool, stirring occasionally to prevent a skin from forming.

Core and slice the apple then sprinkle with lemon juice to prevent discoloration. Cut the cake horizontally. Whip the cream until stiff and reserve a little for piping. Gradually stir in the cornflour mixture to the remaining cream. Chill. Spread the base with some of this mixture, place the second layer on top and cover with the remaining mixture. Sprinkle the cake with the shredded coconut and decorate as shown.

Almond gâteau

3 eggs
200 g/7 oz golden syrup
75 g/3 oz self-raising flour
100 g/4 oz ground almonds
½ teaspoon almond essence
Filling and topping
225 g/8 oz cream cheese
1 (142-ml/5-fl oz) carton of soured cream
3 tablespoons golden syrup
grated rind and juice of 1 lemon
few drops of almond essence
1½ teaspoons gelatine
1 tablespoon hot water
300 ml/½ pint double cream
100 g/4 oz flaked almonds, lightly toasted
few blanched almonds, halved and toasted
few lemon slices, quartered

Whisk the eggs with the golden syrup until pale and creamy. Sieve the flour over the eggs, add the ground almonds and the almond essence and fold in gently using a metal spoon. Turn into a bottom-lined and greased 20-cm/8-inch cake tin and bake in a moderate oven (160°C, 325°F, Gas Mark 3) for 50–55 minutes, or until well risen and golden brown. Turn out removing the greaseproof paper while the cake is hot.
To fill the gâteau Beat together the first five ingredients. Dissolve the gelatine in the hot water in a basin over boiling water. Whisk into the cheese mixture and chill until almost set. Slice the cake and spoon the filling over one half. Place the other half on top.

Whip the cream until stiff and spread a little over the sides of the cake. Press the flaked almonds around the sides using a palette knife. Cover the top of the cake with cream and using a nylon piping bag fitted with a large star nozzle, pipe the remaining cream around the edge of the cake. Decorate with lightly toasted blanched almond halves and lemon.

Brandied chestnut roll

3 eggs
100 g/4 oz castor sugar
2 tablespoons brandy
100 g/4 oz plain flour
Filling and decoration
castor sugar
300 ml/½ pint double cream
1 tablespoon castor sugar
1 (250-g/8¾-oz) can chestnut spread (crème de marrons)
175 g/6 oz plain chocolate
15 g/½ oz butter
2 tablespoons brandy
few marrons glacés (optional)

Whisk the eggs with the sugar until pale and thick. Gently fold in the sieved flour and brandy using a metal spoon. Pour the mixture into a bottom-lined and greased 23 × 33-cm/9 × 13-inch Swiss roll tin and bake in a hot oven (220°C, 425°F, Gas Mark 7) for 10–12 minutes. Cover a clean damp teatowel with a sheet of greaseproof paper sprinkled with a little castor sugar. Turn the cake out on to the paper, carefully remove the greaseproof paper used in cooking and trim the crisp edges off the cake. Make a shallow slit across the width of the cake at one end, place a clean sheet of greaseproof paper over the cake and roll up. Cool on a wire tray.
To fill and decorate the roll Whip the cream with the sugar until stiff, and stir half the cream into the chestnut spread and mix until smooth. Carefully unroll the cake and remove the greaseproof paper. Spread the chestnut cream over the cake and re-roll.

Melt the chocolate with the butter and brandy. Cool, then cover the cake completely. Mark it with a fork when half set. Decorate with the reserved cream and marrons glacés.

Choux gâteau

150 ml/¼ pint water
50 g/2 oz butter
65 g/2½ oz plain flour, sieved
2 eggs
grated rind of 1 orange
25 g/1 oz flaked almonds
Filling and decoration
grated rind of ½ orange
juice of 1 orange
2 tablespoons sweet sherry
1 tablespoon thick honey
300 ml/½ pint double cream
icing sugar

Place the water and butter together in a saucepan and heat gently until the butter melts. Bring rapidly to the boil and add all the flour. Over the heat, beat thoroughly to form a smooth ball. Cool slightly then beat in the eggs individually, together with the orange rind. Place the paste in a nylon piping bag fitted with a 1-cm/½-inch plain nozzle and pipe three small buns on a greased baking tray. Pipe the remaining mixture into a greased 20-cm/8-inch sandwich tin and sprinkle the flaked almonds over the top. Bake the buns in a hot oven (220°C, 425°F, Gas Mark 7) for 10 minutes then reduce the temperature to (190°C, 375°F, Gas Mark 5) and cook for a further 10–15 minutes.

Bake the main gâteau in a moderately hot oven (200°C, 400°F, Gas Mark 6) for 35 minutes then reduce the temperature to (190°C, 375°F, Gas Mark 5) and bake for a further 10–15 minutes. Split both the buns and gâteau immediately and cool on a wire tray.
To fill and decorate the gâteau Stir together all the ingredients except the icing sugar and whip until stiff. Fill the buns with some of the cream then spread the remaining cream over the bottom half of the main gâteau. Place the top half on the cream, arrange the buns in the middle and sieve over a little icing sugar.

Walnut and banana galette

175 g/6 oz butter or margarine
125 g/4 oz castor sugar
grated rind of ½ lemon
175 g/6 oz plain flour
100 g/4 oz walnuts, chopped
Filling and decoration
300 ml/½ pint double cream
2 tablespoons icing sugar
4 bananas

Cream the butter, sugar and lemon rind until light and fluffy. Fold in the flour and knead together into a soft dough. Place in a polythene bag and chill for 30 minutes in the refrigerator.

Divide the dough into three. Grease and flour three baking sheets and mark an 18-cm/7-inch circle on each. Place a piece of dough in each circle and press out flat to fill the circle. Sprinkle the tops with the chopped walnuts and bake in a moderate oven (180°C, 350°F, Gas Mark 4) for 20–25 minutes. Allow to cool before turning out on to a wire tray.
To fill and decorate the galette Whip the cream and fold in the icing sugar. Slice the bananas and sprinkle with a little lemon juice, to prevent discoloration. Sandwich the layers with some cream and bananas. Using a nylon piping bag, pipe cream on top of the galette and decorate with slices of banana. Allow to stand for 30 minutes before serving.

HELPFUL HINT
To mark circles on the floured baking tray, use a saucepan lid as a guide.

Praline gâteau

125 g/4 oz castor sugar
3 eggs
75 g/3 oz plain flour
40 g/1½ oz butter or margarine, melted
grated rind of 1 lemon
Praline
100 g/4 oz split almonds
150 g/5 oz castor sugar
Filling and decoration
300 ml/½ pint double cream

Whisk the sugar and eggs in a basin over a saucepan of hot water until thick and creamy. Remove from the heat; continue to whisk until cool. Sieve the flour and fold into the whisked mixture with the butter and lemon rind, using a metal spoon. Divide the mixture between two bottom-lined and greased 20-cm/8-inch sandwich tins. Bake in a moderately hot oven (180°C, 350°F, Gas Mark 4) for 15–20 minutes. Allow to cool slightly before turning out on to a wire tray.

To make the praline Place the almonds and sugar in a saucepan and allow the sugar to melt over a very low heat. Shake the pan occasionally to allow the syrup to coat the almonds. Cook until the mixture turns a caramel colour. Pour into an oiled tin and allow to set. Crush, using a rolling pin.

To fill and decorate the gâteau Whip the cream and mix sufficient cream and praline together to fill the gâteau. Sandwich the two layers together. Spread a little of the cream around the edge of the gâteau and press the praline on to the sides using a palette knife. Use the remaining cream to spread over the top and, using a nylon piping bag, pipe rosettes. Sprinkle with any remaining praline.

Fresh lime gâteau

50 g/2 oz castor sugar
2 eggs
50 g/2 oz plain flour
grated rind of 1 lime
castor sugar
Filling and decoration
300 ml/½ pint double cream
juice of ½ lime
slices of fresh lime

Whisk the sugar and eggs in a basin over a saucepan of hot water, until the mixture is thick and pale in colour. Remove from the heat and continue to whisk until cool. Sieve the flour twice and fold into the whisked mixture with the rind of the lime. Place the mixture in a bottom-lined and greased 28 × 18-cm/11 × 7-inch Swiss roll tin, smoothing over evenly. Bake in a moderately hot oven (200°C, 400°F, Gas Mark 6) for 8–10 minutes.

Meanwhile, place a clean, damp teatowel on a working surface, lay a sheet of greaseproof paper on top and sprinkle very lightly with castor sugar. Immediately the Swiss roll is cooked, turn out on to the sugared paper. Remove the lining paper and trim off the crusty edges. Make a shallow indentation with a knife along the narrow edge. Lay a sheet of clean greaseproof paper on top of the Swiss roll, then roll up tightly, and cool.

To fill and decorate the gâteau Whip the cream with the lime juice. Carefully unroll the gâteau, and spread with some of the cream. Roll up and cover with the remaining cream reserving some for piping. Use a palette knife to mark a design. Using a nylon piping bag, pipe cream down the centre and along the edges. Decorate with slices of lime.

Redcurrant ice cream gâteau

Ice cream
200 ml/7 fl oz milk
75 g/3 oz castor sugar
1 egg
300 ml/½ pint double cream
450 g/1 lb redcurrants, washed and trimmed
Biscuit base
175 g/6 oz digestive biscuits
50 g/2 oz butter, melted
Decoration
150 ml/¼ pint double cream
few sprigs of redcurrants (optional)

To make the ice cream Place the milk, sugar and egg in a basin and place over a saucepan of hot water. Stir continuously until the custard thickens slightly and coats the back of the spoon. Allow to cool, then stir in the cream. Pour into a rigid, shallow container and freeze until partially frozen. Liquidise and sieve the redcurrants.

Crush the biscuits to fine crumbs and mix with the melted butter. Using half of the biscuits, line the base of a 1-kg/2-lb foil loaf tin, pressing down well. Chill slightly.

Remove the partially frozen ice cream from the freezer and whisk vigorously until liquid again. Stir in the sieved fruit and pour into the biscuit-lined loaf tin. Sprinkle the remaining biscuits on top and return to the freezer until the ice cream has frozen. Turn out on to a serving dish.

To decorate the gâteau Whip the cream and using a nylon piping bag, pipe rosettes on top of the gâteau and decorate with a few sprigs of redcurrants. Allow to soften in the refrigerator for about 1 hour before serving.

Ginger ice cream gâteau

Ice cream
150 ml/¼ pint milk
1 egg
75 g/3 oz castor sugar
50 ml/2 fl oz green ginger wine
300 ml/½ pint double cream
Almond base
3 egg whites
150 g/5 oz castor sugar
50 g/2 oz cornflour
100 g/4 oz ground almonds
Topping
150 ml/¼ pint double cream
4 tablespoons apricot jam, sieved
3 pieces stem ginger, chopped
50 g/2 oz whole almonds, toasted

To make the ice cream Place the milk, egg and sugar in a basin over a saucepan of hot water and cook, stirring continuously, until the custard thickens slightly and coats the back of the spoon. Allow to cool, then stir in the ginger wine and cream. Pour into a rigid, shallow container and freeze until partially frozen.

To make the almond base Whisk the egg whites until stiff. Add the sugar and whisk again until stiff. Gently fold in the cornflour and ground almonds. Bottom-line a baking tray with parchment paper; fill a nylon piping bag fitted with a 1-cm/½-inch plain nozzle with some of the almond mixture. Pipe nine 7.5-cm/2½-inch lengths. Spread the remaining mixture in a 20-cm/8-inch circle and smooth evenly. Bake in a moderate oven (160°C, 325°F, Gas Mark 3) for 20–25 minutes.

When the ice cream is partially frozen remove from the freezer, pour into a bowl and whisk thoroughly until smooth and creamy. Line a 20-cm/8-inch sandwich cake tin with cling film and pour in the ice cream. Return to the freezer until frozen.

To assemble the gâteau Place the almond base on a flat plate. Carefully lift the ice cream out of the tin and peel off the cling film. Place the ice cream on the almond base. Whip the cream and cut each of the almond fingers in half. Using a little of the cream to secure the fingers, place all round the side of the gâteau, with the cut side downwards.

To make the topping Mix the jam, stem ginger and almonds and spread over the ice cream. Pipe a border of cream around the edge. Serve immediately.

Chocolate cheesecake gâteau

Biscuit base
100 g/4 oz chocolate digestive biscuits
50 g/2 oz butter, melted
Filling
225 g/8 oz cream cheese
100 g/4 oz castor sugar
2 eggs, separated
100 g/4 oz plain bitter chocolate, melted
2 teaspoons gelatine
125 ml/¼ pint double cream, whipped
Decoration
150 ml/¼ pint double cream
chocolate curls (see page 120)
icing sugar

To make the biscuit base Crush the biscuits into fine crumbs and stir in the melted butter. Press on to the base of an 18-cm/7-inch spring form tin and chill.

To make the filling Beat the cream cheese until smooth and add the sugar, egg yolks and melted chocolate. Dissolve the gelatine in 2 tablespoons of hot water and add to the cheese mixture. Whisk the egg whites until stiff and fold into the mixture. Then lastly fold in the whipped cream. Pour into the tin and chill until set.

To decorate the gâteau Whip the cream and using a nylon piping bag, pipe a border around the edge. Decorate the centre with chocolate curls and sprinkle with icing sugar.

Avocado cheesecake gâteau

Biscuit base
225 g/8 oz chocolate digestive biscuits
75 g/3 oz butter
Filling
2 ripe avocado pears
juice of ½ lemon
finely grated rind of 1 lemon
100 g/4 oz cream cheese
75 g/3 oz castor sugar
2 teaspoons gelatine
2 egg whites
150 ml/¼ pint double cream, whipped
Decoration
150 ml/¼ pint double cream, whipped

Crush the biscuits into fine crumbs and stir in the melted butter. Press into a 19-cm/7½-inch spring-form tin, to line the base and sides. Chill well.

To make the filling Peel the avocados and remove the stones. Reserve a few slices for decoration and mash the remainder well. Mix with the lemon juice, grated rind, cream cheese and sugar. Beat until smooth. Dissolve the gelatine in 2 tablespoons of hot water and stir into the mixture. Whisk the egg whites until stiff and fold into the mixture with the whipped cream. Pour into the prepared biscuit base and chill thoroughly until set.

To decorate the gâteau Carefully remove from the tin. Using a nylon piping bag fitted with a star-shaped nozzle, pipe a border of cream around the edge of the cake. Decorate with small slices of avocado.

HELPFUL HINT
To crush biscuits, place in a polythene bag and seal the opened end. Crush into crumbs using a rolling pin.

HELPFUL HINT
To prevent discoloration, sprinkle the slices of avocado for decoration with lemon juice.

Apricot gâteau

3 eggs
75 g/3 oz castor sugar
finely grated rind of 1 lemon
pinch of salt
75 g/3 oz plain flour, sieved
Filling and decoration
150 ml/¼ pint double cream
1 tablespoon icing sugar
1 tablespoon apricot liqueur, (optional)
flaked almonds, toasted
225 g/8 oz fresh apricots, halved and poached
4 tablespoons apricot jam, sieved
angelica leaves

Whisk the eggs and sugar together in a basin over a saucepan of hot water until thick and pale in colour. Remove from the heat and continue to whisk until cool. Add the lemon rind, salt and sieved flour and fold in very carefully with a metal spoon. Divide the mixture between two bottom-lined and greased 20-cm/8-inch sandwich tins. Bake in a moderate oven (180°C, 350°F, Gas Mark 4) for 15–20 minutes. Allow to cool for a few minutes before turning out on to a wire tray.

To fill and decorate the gâteau Whip the cream and fold in the icing sugar and apricot liqueur, if liked. Reserve some for piping. Use a little to sandwich the cakes together, and spread the remainder around the sides. Roll the sides of the cake in the flaked almonds. Arrange the halved apricots on top of the cake and glaze with the apricot jam. Using a nylon piping bag, decorate with the reserved cream and the angelica leaves.

Chocolate brandy snap gâteau

3 eggs
75 g/3 oz castor sugar
65 g/2½ oz plain flour
15 g/½ oz cocoa powder
½ teaspoon baking powder
Filling and decoration
300 ml/½ pint double cream
1 (100-g/3.5-oz) packet brandy snaps
ribbon
25 g/1 oz plain chocolate, melted

Place the eggs and sugar in a basin and whisk over a saucepan of hot water until thick and pale in colour. Remove from the heat and continue to whisk until cool. Sieve the flour, cocoa powder and baking powder together and gently fold into the mixture. Divide between two bottom-lined and greased 20-cm/8-inch sandwich tins. Bake in a moderate oven (180°C, 350°F, Gas Mark 4) for 25–30 minutes. Turn out carefully and cool on a wire tray.

To decorate the gâteau Whip the cream and use a little to sandwich the cakes together. Spread a little around the sides, just enough to secure the brandy snaps around the edge of the cake. Tie a ribbon around the outside of the cake. Spread the remaining cream over the top of the cake, swirling with a palette knife. Place the melted chocolate in a greaseproof piping bag with a tiny hole cut in the point and drizzle over the cream and swirl with a skewer.

HELPFUL HINT
To slice the cake, use a serrated knife and cut with a sawing action.

Mocha torte

175 g/6 oz plain chocolate
1 tablespoon strong black coffee
175 g/6 oz butter
175 g/6 oz castor sugar
4 eggs, separated
150 g/5 oz self-raising flour
Filling and icing
apricot jam, sieved
175 g/6 oz plain chocolate
2 tablespoons strong black coffee
175 g/6 oz icing sugar
150 ml/¼ pint double cream

Melt the chocolate and black coffee in a basin over a saucepan of hot water. Allow to cool.

Cream the butter and sugar together until light and fluffy. Gradually beat in the egg yolks and cooled chocolate. Fold in the flour using a metal spoon. Whisk the egg whites until stiff, then fold into the mixture. Pour into a bottom-lined and greased 20-cm/8-inch cake tin and bake in a cool oven (150°C, 300°F, Gas Mark 2) for 1–1½ hours. Allow to cool in the cake tin for 10 minutes before turning out on to a wire tray.
To fill and decorate the torte Cut the cake in half and sandwich together with the sieved apricot jam. Brush the entire cake with a thin layer of the jam. Melt the chocolate and coffee in a basin over a saucepan of hot water, then remove from the heat and beat in the icing sugar. Pour the icing over the cake working it down the sides using a palette knife. Allow to set, then using a nylon piping bag, pipe rosettes of cream on top.

Rum and raisin gâteau

175 g/6 oz butter or margarine
175 g/6 oz castor sugar
2 tablespoons rum
3 eggs
200 g/7 oz self-raising flour
grated rind and juice of 1 orange
175 g/6 oz raisins
Filling and decoration
300 ml/½ pint double cream
2 tablespoons rum
grated rind of 1 orange
1 tablespoon castor sugar
1 orange, sliced

Cream the butter with the sugar and rum until pale and fluffy. Gradually beat in the eggs then sieve the flour over the mixture and fold in using a metal spoon. Carefully fold in the orange rind, juice and raisins. Turn into a lined and greased 1-kg/2-lb loaf tin and bake in a moderate oven (160°C, 325°F, Gas Mark 3) for 1½–1¾ hours, or until browned and firm to the touch. Turn out and cool on a wire tray.
To fill and decorate the gâteau Whip the cream with the rum, orange rind and castor sugar until stiff. Slice the cake into three, vertically along its length and sandwich the three pieces of cake back together with some of the cream. Decorate the cake with the remaining cream, covering it completely and use a round bladed knife to achieve a swirled surface. Arrange the orange slices on top.

HELPFUL HINT
To slice the cake for assembling, place it on a board and with a serrated knife, cut the cake vertically into three portions.

Chapter

5

NOVELTY CAKES

The cakes featured in this chapter are surprisingly easy to make and such fun for children's parties. The bases can be made in advance and frozen and some of the cakes can be frozen, iced, but without the final decorations. Remember to save any left over trimmings. These can be frozen for future use, or used as a base for a trifle.

Humpty Dumpty

225 g/8 oz butter or margarine
225 g/8 oz castor sugar
4 eggs, lightly beaten
175 g/6 oz self-raising flour
1 teaspoon baking powder
75 g/3 oz desiccated coconut
Icing and decoration
225 g/8 oz raspberry jam
100 g/4 oz desiccated coconut
225 g/8 oz butter icing (see page 112)
Smarties
short strip of liquorice
225 g/8 oz almond paste, made-up weight (see page 116)*

*If preferred you can use ready prepared almond paste available from most supermarkets.

Cream the butter and sugar together until light and fluffy. Beat in the eggs. Sieve the flour and baking powder over the mixture and fold in carefully with the coconut using a metal spoon.

Grease a 600-ml/1-pint pudding basin and bottom-line and grease an 18-cm/7-inch square shallow tin. Two-thirds fill the pudding basin with cake mixture and spread the remainder evenly in the square tin. Bake in a moderate oven (160°C, 325°F, Gas Mark 3), the square tin for 25–35 minutes and the basin for 40–50 minutes. Turn out and cool on a wire tray.

To ice and decorate the cake Cut the square cake in half and sandwich together with a little jam to form an oblong cake of 8.5 × 18 cm/3½ × 7 inches. Spread the jam all over the cake and coat completely in coconut. Use a skewer to bring the jam through and give the brick wall effect.

Cover the basin cake completely with the butter icing. Use Smarties for buttons, nose and eyes and place Humpty Dumpty on the wall. Cut a short piece of liquorice and curve it round to form the mouth and eyebrows. Shape arms and legs out of almond paste and place on the cake, using halved, wooden cocktail sticks if necessary.

HELPFUL HINT
To achieve a brick wall effect, use a skewer to mark the coconut.

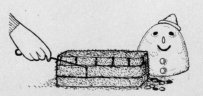

Cuthbert car

1 (23 × 33-cm/9 × 13-inch) sandwich cake (see
boat cake, page 103)
Icing and decoration
1 (25-cm/10-inch) square silver cake board
225 g/8 oz lemon curd
225 g/8 oz butter icing (see page 112)
green food colouring
Smarties
chocolate buttons

To ice and decorate the car Cut the cake in half
widthways and sandwich the two pieces together with
a little of the lemon curd. Place on the cake board. Mix
the remaining lemon curd with the butter icing. Cut out
a piece of greaseproof paper the same size as the cake.
Draw the shape of the car on the paper, place on top
of the cake and use as an outline to cut out the car. Cut
out the wheels from the offcuts.

Reserve 3 tablespoons of the icing and use the
remainder to cover the cake completely. Mark the icing
by using a round bladed knife. Colour the reserved
icing green and pipe the features on the cake using a
greaseproof piping bag with a small hole cut in the
point. Place red and yellow Smarties on the cake to
represent lights and chocolate buttons for hub caps.

HELPFUL HINT
*If a silver cake board is
not available, a thick
piece of cardboard
covered in foil may be
used.*

Bus cake

175 g/6 oz butter or margarine
175 g/6 oz castor sugar
grated rind of 2 lemons
juice of 1 lemon
3 eggs, beaten
225 g/8 oz self-raising flour
Icing and decoration
225 g/8 oz lemon butter icing (see page 112)
yellow food colouring
75 g/3 oz plain chocolate, melted
50 g/2 oz icing sugar
1 tablespoon water
Smarties
2 mini chocolate rolls
100 g/4 oz plain chocolate, grated (optional)

Cream the butter with the sugar and lemon rind until
light and fluffy. Beat in the lemon juice and gradually
beat in the eggs.

Sieve the flour over the mixture and carefully fold in
using a metal spoon. Turn into a lined and greased
1.5-kg/3-lb loaf tin and bake in a moderate oven
(160°C, 325°F, Gas Mark 3) for 1¼–1½ hours. Turn
out and cool on a wire tray. When cool, level off the
top of the cake and cut out a piece of approximately
2.5 × 3.5 cm/1 × 1½ inches from one end of the cake
to form the engine shape.

To ice and decorate the cake Reserve 2 tablespoons
of the butter icing. Colour the remainder yellow and
cover the cake completely. Cream the melted chocolate with the reserved butter icing. Place in a greaseproof piping bag with a tiny hole cut in the point and
pipe the features on the bus. Mix the icing sugar with
the water to give a smooth glacé icing and pipe faces
on the Smarties. Place these in the windows.

Halve the mini rolls and place under the cake to
form wheels. Place on a board and surround with
grated chocolate, if liked.

Chocolate chuffa cake

3 eggs
100 g/4 oz castor sugar
65 g/2½ oz plain flour
25 g/1 oz cocoa powder
castor sugar
Filling
100 g/4 oz chocolate butter icing (see page 112)
Icing and decoration
175 g/6 oz plain chocolate, melted
1 chocolate digestive biscuit
liquorice sweets

Whisk the eggs and sugar together until pale and thick. Sieve the flour and cocoa powder over the mixture and carefully fold in using a metal spoon. Spread evenly over a bottom-lined and greased 23 × 33-cm/9 × 13-inch Swiss roll tin and bake in a hot oven (220°C, 425°F, Gas Mark 7) for 12 minutes.

Turn out on to a sheet of greaseproof paper sprinkled with a little castor sugar. Trim the edges of the cake and make a shallow slit down one of the narrow ends. Place another sheet of greaseproof paper over the cake and carefully roll up. Leave to cool on a wire tray.

To fill, ice and decorate the cake When cold, carefully unroll the cake, remove the greaseproof paper, spread with butter icing then re-roll. Cut a piece approximately 10 cm/4 inches long from one end and coat both pieces in the melted chocolate. Place the biscuit on one end of the bigger piece and leave until set.

Turn the smaller piece up on end and place at the other end of the longer piece of cake. Arrange the liquorice sweets to form wheels and a funnel. Decorate the cake with some of the liquorice sweets and a piece of cotton wool to represent smoke from the funnel.

Boat cake

175 g/6 oz butter or margarine
175 g/6 oz castor sugar
few drops of vanilla essence
3 eggs, lightly beaten
175 g/6 oz self-raising flour
3 tablespoons strawberry jam
Icing and decoration
225 g/8 oz butter icing (see page 112)
red food colouring
1 liquorice sweet
few bought chocolate sticks

Cream the butter and sugar together until light and fluffy. Gradually beat in the vanilla essence with the eggs. Sieve the flour over the mixture and fold in using a metal spoon. Spread evenly over a bottom-lined and greased 23 × 33-cm/9 × 13-inch Swiss roll tin and bake in a moderate oven (180°C, 350°F, Gas Mark 4) for 20–25 minutes. Turn out on to a wire tray, remove the greaseproof paper and leave to cool.

Cut a strip approximately 5 cm/2 inches in width off the narrow edge of the cake. Halve the remaining cake widthwise and sandwich together with most of the jam. Halve the strip along the edge and sandwich together using the remaining jam.

Cut the shape of the boat from the main piece of cake, measuring 13 cm/5 inches wide at one end and shaped to a point at the other. Cut one end of the small piece of cake to a point and place on top of the main cake, to form the cabin.

To ice and decorate the cake Colour half the butter icing red. Reserve 2 tablespoons of each portion of butter icing for piping. Cover the main part of the cake in white butter icing and the cabin in red. Using a greaseproof piping bag with a tiny hole cut in the point, pipe the remaining features on the cake. Place the liquorice sweet as the funnel on top of the cabin and chocolate sticks around the edge.

Windmill cake

375 g/12 oz plain flour
¼ teaspoon salt
225 g/8 oz butter or margarine
25 g/1 oz cocoa powder
100 g/4 oz castor sugar
1 egg yolk
¼ teaspoon almond essence
Icing and decoration
175 g/6 oz butter or margarine
275 g/10 oz icing sugar, sieved
few drops of almond essence
1 tablespoon cocoa powder
2 teaspoons boiling water
50 g/2 oz chocolate, grated
100 g/4 oz plain chocolate, melted
3 tablespoons icing sugar, sieved
¾ teaspoon boiling water
liquorice sweets
Smarties
almond paste (optional)

Sieve the flour and salt into a bowl. Add the butter and rub into the flour until the mixture resembles fine breadcrumbs. Add the sieved cocoa powder and sugar then mix to a dough with the egg yolk and almond essence. Form the dough into a roll of approximately 7.5 cm/3 inches in diameter, wrap in cling film and chill until firm.

Cut into approximately eight slices and bake on a greased baking sheet in a moderately hot oven (190°C, 375°F, Gas Mark 5) for 15–20 minutes. Cool on a wire tray.

To ice and decorate the cake Cream the butter with the icing sugar until pale and fluffy. Divide the creamed mixture into two portions and flavour one with almond essence. Cream the cocoa powder with the boiling water and use to flavour the remaining cream. Add the grated chocolate to the chocolate cream.

Sandwich the cooled biscuits together with the chocolate cream to form a tall pile. Chill until firm. Cover the outside completely with the almond cream.

Draw the shape of the sails on a piece of greaseproof paper. Carefully spread the melted chocolate within the outline leaving a small hole in the middle. Keep the layer even, not too thin and as smooth as possible. Similarly, draw and make chocolate windows and a door. Leave the chocolate shapes until firm and chill for an hour.

Mix the icing sugar with the water to give a smooth icing. Using a greaseproof piping bag with a tiny hole cut in the point, pipe the outline of the slats on the sails and the panes on the windows. When completely dry, carefully place one or two liquorice sweets on the end of a cocktail stick and use to attach the sails to the cake. Place the door and windows on the windmill. Arrange the Smarties on the top of the cake.

Make almond paste flowers to put around the windmill, if liked.

Variation
If preferred, the windows and door may be made from almond paste (see page 116). Roll it out thinly and cut out the required shapes. The almond paste can also be tinted, before rolling out, with food colouring.

HELPFUL HINT
For quickness, this cake can be made using bought digestive biscuits and the sails can be made of cardboard instead of chocolate.

Treasure chest

175 g/6 oz butter or margarine
175 g/6 oz castor sugar
grated rind of 2 oranges
3 eggs
200 g/7 oz self-raising flour
juice of 1 orange
Icing and decoration
175 g/6 oz plain chocolate
50 g/2 oz butter
100 g/4 oz orange butter icing (see page 112)
variety of small sweets

Cream the butter with the sugar until pale and fluffy. Carefully beat in the orange rind and eggs. Sieve the flour over the mixture and fold in gently using a metal spoon. Lastly, fold in the orange juice. Turn into a lined and greased 1-kg/2-lb loaf tin and bake in a moderate oven (160°C, 325°F, Gas Mark 3) for approximately 1½ hours. Turn out and cool on a wire tray.

To ice and decorate the cake Melt the chocolate with the butter in a basin over a pan of hot water. Slice the top off the cake and reserve as the lid. Cover the whole of the cake thinly with the chocolate. When the chocolate is set, place the butter icing in a piping bag fitted with a small star nozzle and pipe an edge around the cake. Pipe designs around the sides and top of the cake. Place the various sweets as 'treasure' on top of the cake, arranging some to hang over the edge. Arrange the lid, tilting slightly backwards, on the top of the cake.

Book cake

1 (23 × 33-cm/9 × 13-inch) sandwich cake (see boat cake, page 103)
Icing and decoration
225 g/8 oz butter icing (see page 112)
50 g/2 oz plain chocolate, melted
1 piece of coloured ribbon

To ice and decorate the cake Cover the cake completely in butter icing, reserving about one third for piping. Place the reserved butter icing in a piping bag fitted with a small star nozzle and pipe the edges around the cake. Use a small greaseproof piping bag with a tiny hole cut in its point to pipe the features on the cake in melted chocolate to resemble a book. Arrange the ribbon down the middle of the cake to form a book mark.

HELPFUL HINT
Before icing the cake, place it on a large board or tray.

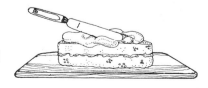

Log cabin

350 g/12 oz butter or margarine
350 g/12 oz castor sugar
6 eggs, lightly beaten
300 g/11 oz self-raising flour
50 g/2 oz cocoa powder
Icing and decoration
225 g/8 oz chocolate butter icing (see page 112)
2 (100-g/3.53-oz) packets chocolate
finger biscuits
100 g/4 oz almond paste made-up weight (see
page 116)*
2 tablespoons icing sugar, sieved
¾ teaspoon water
red food colouring
liquorice sweet

*If preferred, you can use ready prepared almond paste available from most supermarkets.

Cream the butter and sugar together until light and fluffy. Gradually beat in the eggs together with 2 tablespoons of the flour. Sieve the remaining flour and cocoa powder over the mixture and fold in using a metal spoon.

Spread the mixture evenly over a lined and greased 20-cm/8-inch square cake tin. Bake in a moderate oven (160°C, 325°F, Gas Mark 3) for 2 hours. Turn out on to a wire tray, remove the greaseproof paper and leave to cool.

To ice and decorate the cake When cool, cut the top of the cake level if necessary then cut one third of the cake off the end to use for the roof. Cut the smaller piece of cake through diagonally to form two triangular shaped pieces. Reserve 2 tablespoons of the butter icing for piping. Cover the top of the main piece of cake with butter icing and place the two pieces, ends together, on top for the roof. Cover the cake completely with butter icing, using slightly less on the roof

than the sides.

Arrange the chocolate finger biscuits on the roof to resemble logs. Mark the sides of the cake horizontally using a round bladed knife to give the effect of a log cabin. Roll out the almond paste and cut out a door and windows. Mix the icing sugar with the water to form a thick glacé icing. Paint the door using a fine paintbrush with the food colouring and using a greaseproof piping bag with a tiny hole cut in the point, pipe glacé icing for the features. Place a liquorice sweet on top of the roof for the chimney. Sieve a little icing sugar on to the roof to represent snow.

Variation

For a nutty cake, omit the cocoa powder and use 350 g/12 oz self-raising flour. Fold in 100 g/4 oz chopped walnuts with the remaining flour. Bake as for the chocolate cake.

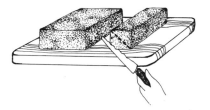

HELPFUL HINT
To form the roof, cut one third off the cake and cut the smaller piece diagonally to form two triangular shapes.

Chocolate hedgehogs

MAKES 6

225 g/8 oz plain flour
100 g/4 oz butter or margarine
75 g/3 oz castor sugar
grated rind of 2 oranges
3 tablespoons orange juice
275 g/10 oz chocolate cake crumbs
3 tablespoons lemon jelly marmalade, warmed
50 g/2 oz butter, melted
1 tablespoon chocolate, melted
5 tablespoons orange juice
Icing and decoration
50 g/2 oz blanched almonds
225 g/8 oz plain chocolate, melted

Sieve the flour into a bowl, add the butter and rub in lightly until the mixture resembles fine breadcrumbs. Add the sugar and orange rind and mix to form a dough using the orange juice.

Knead lightly then roll out to 5 mm/¼ inch thickness. Cut out six oval shapes measuring 10 × 6 cm/4 × 2½ inches. Place on greased baking trays and bake in a moderately hot oven (190°C, 375°F, Gas Mark 5) for 12–15 minutes. Cool on a wire tray.

Meanwhile, mix together the remaining ingredients. Chill until the mixture is firm enough to shape with the hands. Pile this mixture on top of the cooled orange bases and smooth into domes. Shape the front to form noses. Chill until firm.

To ice and decorate the cakes Quarter the almonds lengthwise and stick into the hedgehogs to resemble spines. Reserve a few pieces of the almonds for eyes and noses. Coat the hedgehogs completely in melted chocolate and leave until firm. When the chocolate is half set, place small pieces of almond on the front to form eyes and a nose.

Ladybird cakes

MAKES 10

225 g/8 oz plain flour
175 g/6 oz butter or margarine
100 g/4 oz castor sugar
25 g/1 oz cocoa powder
1 egg yolk
350 g/12 oz cake crumbs
225 g/8 oz raspberry jam, warmed
2 tablespoons lemon juice
25 g/1 oz butter, melted
Icing and decoration
225 g/8 oz butter icing (see page 112)
red food colouring
chocolate dots
100 g/4 oz plain chocolate, melted

Sieve the flour into a bowl, add the butter and rub in lightly until the mixture resembles fine breadcrumbs. Add the sugar and cocoa powder then mix to a dough using the egg yolk. Knead lightly and roll out to approximately 5 mm/¼ inch thickness. Cut out ten ovals measuring approximately 7.5 × 6 cm/3 × 2½ inches. Place on greased baking trays and bake in a moderately hot oven (190°C, 375°F, Gas Mark 5) for 12–15 minutes. Cool on a wire tray.

Mix together the remaining ingredients. Chill until firm enough to shape with the hands. Pile this on top of the biscuit bases and smooth into domes. Chill until firm.

To ice and decorate the cakes Colour the butter icing with the red food colouring and use to cover the ladybirds. Cover two-thirds of the cakes with the chocolate dots and use for eyes and nose. Place the melted chocolate in a greaseproof piping bag with a tiny hole cut in the point and pipe the wing features on to the cakes. Leave until completely set.

Merry maypole cake

1 (20-cm/8-inch) Victoria sandwich cake (see
page 20)
Icing and decoration
350 g/12 oz butter icing (see page 112)
pink or blue food colouring
50 g/2 oz chocolate vermicelli
coloured ribbons
coloured drinking straw
wooden figures or jelly babies

To ice and decorate the cake Sandwich the cake
together with a little of the butter icing. Colour the
remaining butter icing either pink or blue. Reserve one
third of the butter icing for piping. Spread the sides of
the cake thinly with some butter icing. Sprinkle the
chocolate vermicelli on a piece of greaseproof paper
and holding the cake carefully on its side, roll the sides
of the cake in the strands until completely coated.

Place the cake on a board or plate and spread the
top with the remaining butter icing. Place the reserved
butter icing in a piping bag fitted with a small star or
rosette nozzle and pipe the edging on the cake.

Stick the straw in the middle of the cake and attach
the ribbons to it using a wire tie. Carefully secure the
other ends of the ribbons to the wooden figures or jelly
babies either with a little buttercream or by tying them.

Chocolate clock cake

1 (20-cm/8-inch) chocolate Victoria sandwich
cake (see page 20)
Icing and decoration
225 g/8 oz fudge icing (see page 114)
50 g/2 oz icing sugar
about 1 tablespoon hot water
chocolate buttons
50 g/2 oz plain chocolate, melted
ribbon

To ice and decorate the cake Sandwich the cake
together using one third of the fudge icing. Spread the
remaining icing over the top and sides of the cake.

Sieve the icing sugar into a small basin and mix
gradually with the water to give a smooth icing. Using a
greaseproof piping bag with a tiny hole cut in the point,
pipe the numbers 1 to 12 on the chocolate buttons and
a spiral on the button that is to go in the middle of the
cake. Place the buttons around the edge of the cake to
resemble a clock and the one with the spiral in the
middle.

Draw the shape of the hands for the clock on a piece
of greaseproof paper. Carefully spread the melted
chocolate within the outline of the drawing, making it
as thick and smooth as possible. Leave in a cool place
until set.

Tie a ribbon around the side of the cake and place
the hands on the clock face, pointing them to the
number which is appropriate for the age of the child
whose birthday is being celebrated or any other
number which is relevant to the celebration.

Numeral cake

1 (20-cm/8-inch) Victoria sandwich cake (see
page 20)
Icing and decoration
450 g/1 lb butter icing (see page 112)
food colouring
coloured sweets or chocolate buttons
candles

Cut out two 20-cm/8-inch rounds of greaseproof
paper, overlap slightly at one end and pin together.
Draw the shape of the figure 3 on the two pieces of
paper and mark a dotted line at the point where they
overlap. Use as much of the area as possible when
drawing the numeral. Unpin the pieces of paper and
cut out the shapes which have been drawn. Use these
as a pattern to cut out the shape from the two pieces of
cake.
To ice and decorate the cake Fit the cake together on
a board. Colour the butter cream as wished. Reserve a
quarter of the butter cream for piping and use
remainder to cover the cake completely. Using a
greaseproof piping bag fitted with a small rosette or
star nozzle, pipe an edge around the cake. Decorate
with the sweets and place the appropriate number of
candles on the cake.

Variations

Using the same method, that is cutting out paper
patterns first, other numerals may be cut out of the
cake. For some of the smaller numbers, the cake may
be sandwiched together first. A figure eight may simply
be made by cutting out a 7.5-cm/3-inch round from
the middle of each piece of cake. The ends of the two
pieces should be cut off slightly where they fit together.
A figure six may be cut out of the cake which has
already been sandwiched together.

Alphabet stack

1 (23 × 33-cm/9 × 13-inch) sandwich cake (see
boat cake, page 103)
Icing and decoration
175 g/6 oz plain chocolate
100 g/4 oz butter or margarine
225 g/8 oz icing sugar, sieved
1–2 tablespoons lemon juice
100 g/4 oz almond paste, made-up weight, (see
page 116)*
food colouring

**If preferred, you can use ready prepared almond paste
available from most supermarkets.*

To ice and decorate the cake Trim the edges off the
cake. Melt the chocolate and butter together. Gradually beat in the icing sugar and lemon juice to give an
icing of a soft consistency, similar to that of a firm
butter icing. Add a little more lemon juice if necessary.
The icing will need vigorous beating to obtain a soft
consistency and will harden as it cools.

Spread the icing over the top of the cake and leave
until almost set. Using a sharp, wet knife, cut the cake
into four, both widthways and lengthways, to give
sixteen pieces of cake.

Knead the almond paste slightly then roll out thinly
on a clean surface sprinkled with sieved icing sugar.
Using a small, sharp pointed knife cut out the almond
paste in the shape of the letters, making them approximately 3.5–5 cm/1½–2 inches in height. Using a small
artist's paint brush or pastry brush, colour the letters
with various diluted food colours. Leave until dry, then
place on the pieces of cake and leave until the icing is
quite firm. Arrange in a stack or in the name of a child.

111

ICING AND DECORATION

With the clear and precise step-by-step instructions detailed in this chapter, you'll be able to achieve a professional finish on all your decorated cakes. Turn melted chocolate into chocolate leaves, or royal icing into moulded flowers to give that final professional touch and to impress your friends with your masterpieces.

Butter icing

MAKES 225 g/8 oz BUTTER ICING, SUFFICIENT TO FILL AND ICE THE TOP AND SIDES OF A 20-cm/8-inch SANDWICH CAKE.

75 g/3 oz butter or margarine
225 g/8 oz icing sugar
2 tablespoons milk
food colouring (optional)

Place all the ingredients in a mixing bowl and beat together with a wooden spoon until well mixed.

Variations
Orange or lemon icing Substitute the milk for orange or lemon juice.

Coffee icing Replace 1 tablespoon milk with 1 table-spoon coffee essence or 1 tablespoon instant coffee dissolved in 1 tablespoon boiling water. Cool before adding to the icing.

Chocolate icing Replace 1 tablespoon milk with 1 tablespoon cocoa powder blended with 2 tablespoons hot water.

Mocha icing Add 1 tablespoon coffee essence and 1 tablespoon cocoa powder blended with 2 tablespoons hot water.

Basket cake

1 Victoria sandwich, made with
175 g/6 oz butter or margarine
175 g/6 oz castor sugar
3 eggs
175 g/6 oz self-raising flour (see page 20)
Icing and decoration
350 g/12 oz chocolate butter icing (see opposite)
1 (23-cm/9-inch) silver cake board
sweets

Make up the Victoria sandwich cake, as directed, and place in a lined and greased 20-cm/8-inch cake tin. Bake in a moderate oven (160°C, 325°F, Gas Mark 3) for 1–1¼ hours. Turn out and cool on a wire tray.

Cut a slice horizontally across the top of the cake to form the lid.

To ice and decorate the cake Make up the chocolate butter icing as directed. Place the cake on the silver cake board and cover with a thin layer of the icing. Fill two greaseproof piping bags with the icing, one fitted with a plain writing nozzle and the other with a ribbon nozzle. Holding the ribbon nozzle sideways on to the cake, pipe three lines evenly spaced one above the other and all the same length. Pipe a vertical line using the writing tube along the edge of the basket weaving. Continue this process until the cake is covered. Cover the outer edge of the lid in the same way. Arrange the lid at an angle on top of the cake to form an open basket. Fill the inside with sweets.

Fudge icing

MAKES 225 g/8 oz OF FUDGE ICING SUFFICIENT TO
FILL AND ICE THE TOP AND SIDES OF A 20-cm/8-inch
SANDWICH CAKE

**50 g/2 oz butter or margarine
3 tablespoons milk
225 g/8 oz icing sugar, sieved**

Place all the ingredients in a basin over a saucepan of
hot water. Stir until smooth and glossy. Remove from
the heat and allow to cool. Beat well with a wooden
spoon until the mixture is thick enough to spread.

Variations
Lemon or orange fudge icing Replace 2 tablespoons
milk with 2 tablespoons orange or lemon juice.

Coffee fudge icing Replace 1 tablespoon milk with 1
tablespoon instant coffee dissolved in 1 tablespoon
boiling water.

Chocolate fudge icing Use only 1 tablespoon milk and
2 tablespoons hot water blended with 1 tablespoon
cocoa powder.

Glacé icing

MAKES 225 g/8 oz GLACÉ ICING, SUFFICIENT TO ICE
18–20 SMALL CAKES OR THE TOP OF A 20-cm/8-inch
CAKE.

**225 g/8 oz icing sugar, sieved
2–3 tablespoons water
food colouring (optional)**

Place all the ingredients in a mixing bowl and beat with
a wooden spoon until smooth.

Variations
Orange, lemon or lime glacé icing Replace the water
with fresh fruit juice or squash.

Coffee glacé icing Replace 1 tablespoon of the water
with 1 tablespoon coffee essence or 1 teaspoon instant
coffee dissolved in 1 tablespoon hot water.

Chocolate glacé icing Sieve 2 tablespoons cocoa
powder with the icing sugar, adding a little more water
if necessary.

To feather-ice a cake Remove a few teaspoonfuls of
the icing and add a few drops of food colouring. Place
in a greaseproof piping bag fitted with a small, plain
writing nozzle. Pour the remaining icing over the top of
the cake and spread evenly with a palette knife. Pipe
parallel rows of the reserved icing on top and using a
skewer, drag the point across the rows of icing to give a
feathered effect.

Fondant icing

MAKES 350 g/12 oz FONDANT ICING, SUFFICIENT TO
COVER AN 18-cm/7-inch ROUND OR A 15-cm/6-inch
SQUARE CAKE

**350 g/12 oz icing sugar, sieved
1 egg white
1 tablespoon liquid glucose, warmed
icing sugar
egg white, to brush cake**

Place the icing sugar, egg white and glucose in a
mixing bowl and mix together using a palette knife.
Knead together with the fingertips until the dough is
formed. Turn out on to a board well dredged with icing
sugar and knead until easy to handle.

Roll out the dough approximately 5 cm/2 inches
larger than the surface of the cake to be iced. Brush the
cake with egg white. Place the icing on top of the cake
and smooth the icing quickly using fingers dipped in
cornflour, easing the icing down the sides of the cake.
Trim the icing at the base and allow to harden before
decorating. Do not store in an airtight tin.

This icing can be used for moulding decorations and
flowers.

American frosting

MAKES 175 g/6 oz AMERICAN FROSTING, SUFFICIENT
TO FILL AND ICE THE TOP AND SIDES OF A 20-cm/8-
inch SANDWICH CAKE

**1 egg white
175 g/6 oz icing sugar
1 tablespoon golden syrup
3 tablespoons water
pinch of salt
1 teaspoon lemon juice**

Place all the ingredients in a basin over a saucepan of
hot water and whisk until the icing stands in peaks.
Remove from the heat and continue whisking until the
mixture has cooled. Spread over the cake using a
palette knife.

This frosting must be used as soon as it is made.

Almond paste chart for rich fruit cakes

	12 cm/5 in ○ 10 cm/4 in □	15 cm/6 in ○ 12 cm/5 in □	18 cm/7 in ○ 15 cm/6 in □	20 cm/8 in ○ 18 cm/7 in □	23 cm/9 in ○ 20 cm/8 in □	25 cm/10 in ○ 23 cm/9 in □	28 cm/11 in ○ 25 cm/10 in □	30 cm/12 in ○ 28 cm/11 in □	32 cm/13 in ○ 30 cm/12 in □
GROUND ALMONDS	125 g/4 oz	175 g/6 oz	225 g/8 oz	350 g/12 oz	450 g/1 lb	575 g/1¼ lb	675 g/1½ lb	850 g/1 lb 14 oz	1 kg/2 lb
ICING SUGAR	50 g/2 oz	75 g/3 oz	125 g/4 oz	175 g/6 oz	225 g/8 oz	275 g/10 oz	350 g/12 oz	425 g/15 oz	450 g/1 lb
CASTOR SUGAR	50 g/2 oz	75 g/3 oz	125 g/4 oz	175 g/6 oz	225 g/8 oz	275 g/10 oz	350 g/12 oz	425 g/15 oz	450 g/1 lb
LEMON JUICE	½ tea-spoon	½ tea-spoon	1 tea-spoon	1 tea-spoon	2 tea-spoons	2 tea-spoons	3 tea-spoons	3 tea-spoons	4 tea-spoons
ALMOND ESSENCE	few drops according to taste	few drops according to taste	few drops according to taste	few drops according to taste	few drops according to taste	few drops according to taste	few drops according to taste	few drops according to taste	few drops according to taste
ORANGE FLOWER WATER	few drops according to taste	few drops according to taste	few drops according to taste	few drops according to taste	few drops according to taste	few drops according to taste	few drops according to taste	few drops according to taste	few drops according to taste
EGGS	½	½	1	1	1	2	2–3	3	3

These quantities are sufficient to cover both the top and sides of the cake.

To make the almond paste Place the ground almonds, icing and castor sugar in a mixing bowl and mix together. Add the lemon juice, almond essence, orange flower water and sufficient beaten egg to form a stiff but manageable paste. Knead together with the fingers and place on a board dusted with icing sugar. Knead gently until smooth.

To cover a cake with almond paste Roll out one-third of the almond paste, large enough to cover the top of the cake. Brush the top of the cake with sieved apricot jam and place the almond paste on top (see picture above). Trim level with the sides. Roll out the remaining almond paste into either one long strip, the width of the sides, or two shorter strips, according to the size of the cake. Use string to measure the length. Brush the sides with apricot jam and cover with the almond paste, sealing the edges with a palette knife (see picture above). Leave the cake in a cool, dry place to dry out for 1–2 weeks before icing.

Royal icing chart for rich fruit cakes

	12 cm/5 in ○ 10 cm/4 in □	15 cm/6 in ○ 12 cm/5 in □	18 cm/7 in ○ 15 cm/6 in □	20 cm/8 in ○ 18 cm/7 in □	23 cm/9 in ○ 20 cm/8 in □	25 cm/10 in ○ 23 cm/9 in □	28 cm/11 in ○ 25 cm/10 in □	30 cm/12 in ○ 28 cm/11 in □	32 cm/13 in ○ 30 cm/12 in □
EGG WHITES	2	2	2	3	4	4	4	5	5
ICING SUGAR (SIEVED)	450 g/1 lb	450 g/1 lb	450 g/1 lb	675 g/1½ lb	1 kg/2 lb	1 kg/2 lb	1 kg/2 lb	1.25 kg/ 2½ lb	1.25 kg/ 2½ lb
GLYCERINE	1 tea-spoon	1 tea-spoon	1 tea-spoon	1½ tea-spoons	2 tea-spoons	2 tea-spoons	2 tea-spoons	2½ tea-spoons	2½ tea-spoons
ROSE WATER	few drops to taste	few drops to taste	few drops to taste	few drops to taste	few drops to taste	few drops to taste	few drops to taste	few drops to taste	few drops to taste

These quantities are sufficient to flat ice both the top and sides of the cake. Additional icing will be required for piping, according to the design chosen.

To make the royal icing Place the egg whites in a mixing bowl and whisk until just frothy. Gradually add the icing sugar, beating well between each addition, until the icing is shiny and very white. The consistency of the icing should be thin enough to spread but thick enough to hold its shape when lifted with a spoon. Lastly, beat in the glycerine and rose water. Keep icing in an airtight container. It will keep for up to 4 weeks.

To flat ice a cake Secure the cake to the cake board with a little royal icing and allow to set. Place the cake on a turntable or on an upturned plate. Place a quantity of the icing on top of the cake and spread it over the top with a palette knife, working out any air bubbles. Do not let any of the icing run down the sides. Remove the cake from the turntable and place on the table. Using a metal rule, hold at an angle and draw firmly across the top of the cake (see picture above). Remove the icing from the rule immediately. Trim the icing from the edges of the cake with a palette knife. Leave to harden before icing the sides.

To ice the sides of the cake Replace the cake on the turntable or upturned plate and spread icing on to the sides of the cake with a palette knife. If you are icing a square cake, ice the two opposite sides and allow to dry, before icing the remaining sides. In this way you will achieve good square corners. Holding a plastic scraper at an angle on the sides of the cake, pull right round in one continuous movement, keeping your hand holding the scraper completely still (see picture above). Leave to harden.

If necessary, use a piece of fine sandpaper to sand off any rough edges. Repeat these layers of icing until you have completed 3 or 4 layers and the surface is completely smooth.

Piping royal icing designs

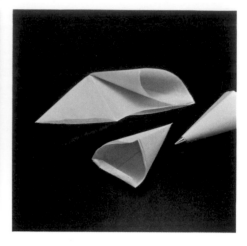

Fold a 20-cm/8-inch square of greaseproof paper in half to form a triangle.

To make a piping bag
With the wider edge of the triangle facing you, fold up the two outer corners to the central point at the top, making a crease along the fold lines.

Form into a cone shape, making sure the point is very firm. Staple or fold the open ends of the bag to secure. Cut off the tip of the cone and insert the piping nozzle.

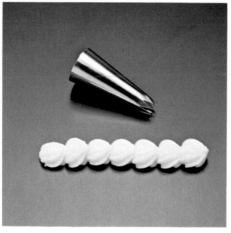

Stars Fit the piping bag with a star nozzle and hold vertically over the cake. Pipe out the stars and when the required size is reached, quickly lift the icing bag off to form a peak.

Designs using a star tube
Shells Hold the piping bag at an angle on the cake in the direction that you are moving. Squeeze the bag in short bursts to form a shell design.

Coils Hold the piping bag at an angle on the cake and pipe in a continuous circular movement to form a coil.

Piping royal icing designs

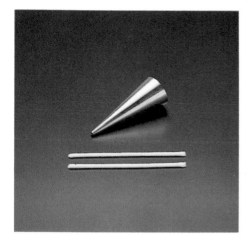

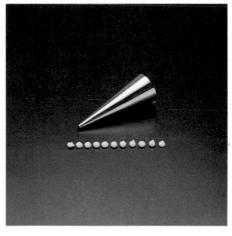

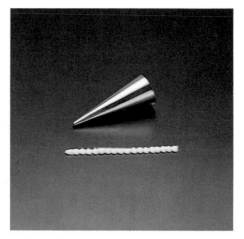

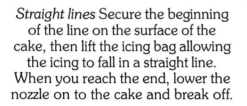

Straight lines Secure the beginning of the line on the surface of the cake, then lift the icing bag allowing the icing to fall in a straight line. When you reach the end, lower the nozzle on to the cake and break off.

Designs using a plain writing nozzle
Beads Hold the icing bag vertically over the cake and press gently to form the required size. Pull away quickly so as not to draw the icing into a point.

Continuous rope beading Hold the icing bag slightly at an angle to the cake and press gently. Do not break off in between each bead but make the design continuous.

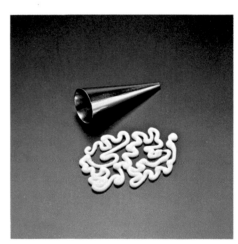

Writing Prick out the lettering on the cake with a pin. Make sure icing is soft and pliable enough to allow it to flow. If writing is to be coloured, pipe in white first and then colour with a small paint brush.

Designs using a plain writing nozzle
Trellis Pipe parallel lines in one direction then allow to dry before piping lines in the opposite direction. Repeat these layers until you reach the required height of trellis. Finish off the last layer with a very fine writing nozzle.

Scribbling This is a simple yet effective way of icing. Hold the icing bag directly on to the cake, keeping the nozzle in contact with the cake all the time and pipe in continuous circular movements.

Chocolate decorations

Melt the chocolate in a basin over a saucepan of hot water. Wash and thoroughly dry the rose leaves.

Chocolate leaves
Using a fine paint brush, coat the underside of the leaves with a layer of melted chocolate. Leave in the refrigerator to harden.

Carefully peel the leaves off the chocolate and keep in the refrigerator until required.

Choose chocolate that is not too brittle and a sharp knife with a straight blade.

Chocolate curls
Hold the blade of the knife at an angle to the block of chocolate and firmly shave a layer off to form a curl.

Repeat until you have the required number of curls. Keep in the refrigerator until needed.

Chocolate decorations

Melt the chocolate in a basin over a saucepan of hot water. Spread out thinly on to waxed or greaseproof paper. Leave to set until just firm.

Chocolate shapes using cutters
Use cutters to cut out a variety of shapes. Keep the trimmings to melt down again.

Take care not to handle the cut out shapes too much as they will loose their gloss. Keep in the refrigerator until required.

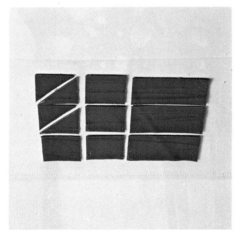

Melt the chocolate in a basin over a saucepan of hot water. Spread out thinly on to waxed or greaseproof paper. Leave to set until just firm.

Chocolate shapes without cutters
Using a ruler as a guide, cut the chocolate into a square with a sharp knife.

Cut into smaller squares which can be halved to form triangles. Keep in the refrigerator until needed.

Crystallised flowers

Mix 15 g/½ oz gum arabic with 2 tablespoons rose water and shake well in a screw top jar. Leave for 2 hours.
Make sure flowers are completely dry and unblemished.

Using a fine paint brush, paint the flower petals all over with the gum arabic solution. Leave until the solution has been absorbed, then sprinkle all over with castor sugar.

Remove any surplus sugar and sprinkle again with sugar if required. Leave to dry and flowers will then become hard.

Runouts

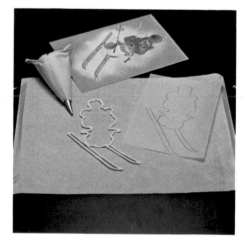  

Trace the chosen design on to waxed or greaseproof paper. Lay the paper on a flat board and secure. Lay a piece of waxed paper on top. Make up the royal icing and pipe along the outline using a greaseproof piping bag fitted with a writing nozzle. Allow to dry slightly.

With a slightly softer royal icing, flood the centre of the runout, using a cocktail stick to guide the icing into all the corners. Allow to harden. It is preferable to use icing without glycerine.

Carefully lift the runout off the paper. Paint the features using food colouring and a fine paint brush. Allow to dry before placing on the cake. Greeting cards are ideal for designing ones own runouts.

Piped roses

Make sure the royal icing is of a consistency that will keep its shape. Using a greaseproof piping bag fitted with a petal shape nozzle, pipe the centre of the rose around the point of a cocktail stick.

Twisting the cocktail stick between the thumb and the first finger, pipe the petals individually until the rose reaches the required size.

Push the bottom of the cocktail stick through a hole in a small piece of card to remove the flower. Allow to harden before using.

Moulded flowers

Press small pieces of fondant icing between your fingers which have been dipped in cornflour. Shape into individual petals. Roll the first petal to form the centre of the rose.

Mould each petal around the centre and build up into a rose. Cut off at the base of the rose if the petals have become too thick. Allow to harden.

Highlight the centre of the rose with food colouring using a fine paint brush. Allow to dry before using.

INDEX

Almond:
Almond clusters 63
Almond gâteau 91
Almond macaroons 63
Almond and orange puffs 54
Almond paste 116
Almond tuiles 50
Alphabet stack 111
American frosting 115
Apple:
Apple and ginger rings 49
Autumn gâteau 90
Cider apple cake 29
Apricot gâteau 98
Apricot and orange teabread 43
Aromatic teabread 40
Austrian coffee gâteau 85
Autumn gâteau 90
Avocado cheesecake gâteau 96

Banana cake 29
Banana date fingers 60
Basket cake 112
Battenburg 20
Birthday cakes 81
Biscuit cups 50
Biscuits see Small cakes and biscuits
Black Forest gâteau 85
Boat cake 103
Boiled fruit cake 36
Bonfire cake 79
Book cake 106
Brandied chestnut roll 91
Brandy snaps 50
Brazilian teabread 41
Brownies 59
Bus cake 102
Butter icing 112
Butterscotch and lemon loaf 38

Cake tins 14; to line 15
Chequered chocolate cake 22
Cherry:
Black Forest gâteau 85
Cherry Madeira cake 26
Chestnut roll, brandied 91
Chocolate:
Brownies 59
Chequered chocolate cake 22
Chocolate and almond cake 39
Chocolate brandy snap gâteau 98
Chocolate butter icing 112
Chocolate cheesecake gâteau 96
Chocolate chuffa cake 103
Chocolate clock cake 110
Chocolate cup cakes 46
Chocolate curls 120
Chocolate decorations 120-1
Chocolate fudge icing 114

Chocolate glacé icing 114
Chocolate hedgehogs 108
Chocolate layer cake 25
Chocolate leaves 120
Chocolate marble squares 57
Chocolate piggy cake 80
Chocolate pistachio loaf 44
Chocolate shortbread hearts 55
Chocolate snowman 72
Chocolate truffle cake 39
Devil's food cake 25
Minted chocolate marble loaf 45
Minty chocolate cups 48
Choux gâteau 92
Christening cake 69
Christmas cakes:
Chocolate snowman 72
Christmas tree 74
Father Christmas 72
Fondant-iced Christmas cake 71
Ski cake 70
Snow-peaked cake 71
Cider apple cake 29
Cinnamon rings 61
Coconut crisps 59
Coconut fudge slices 52
Coconut and lemon cake 26
Coffee See also Mocha
Austrian coffee gâteau 85
Coffee butter icing 112
Coffee butterflies 64
Coffee fudge icing 114
Coffee glacé icing 114
Coffee and pear cake 23
Crunchy coffee cakes 57
Hazelnut coffee cake 22
Spiced coffee teabread 45
Walnut coffee cake 22
Walnut coffee trumpets 61
Creamy peach meringue 88
Crystallised flowers 122
Crystallised fruit cake 34
Cuthbert car 102

Date and pineapple loaf 44
Devil's food cake 25
Dundee cake 34

Easter chick 77
Eighteenth birthday cake 81
Evil witches 78

Fairy cakes 46
Farmhouse loaf 33
Father Christmas 72
Flapjack 53
Florentines 50
Flowers, crystallised 122; moulded 123

Fondant-iced Christmas cake 71
Fondant icing 115; moulded flowers in 123
Freezing cakes 17
Fruit cakes See also Christmas and Wedding Cakes
Boiled fruit cake 36
Crystallised fruit cake 34
Dundee cake 34
Fruit 'n' nut cake 33
Guinness cake 37
Harvest fruit cake 37
Little fruit cakes 46
Nutty fruit round 58
Rich fruit cake 32
Simnel cake 77
Fruity bran fingers 60
Fruity gingerbread 27
Fruity oatcakes 62
Fudge icing 114

Gâteaux:
Almond gâteau 91
Apricot gâteau 98
Austrian coffee gâteau 85
Autumn gâteau 90
Avocado cheesecake gâteau 96
Black Forest gâteau 85
Brandied chestnut roll 91
Chocolate brandy snap gâteau 98
Chocolate cheesecake gâteau 96
Choux gâteau 92
Creamy peach meringue 88
Fresh lime gâteau 93
Ginger ice cream gâteau 95
Hazelnut cream bombe 82
Honey hazelnut gâteau 86
Loganberry gâteau 90
Minted lemon gâteau 86
Mocha roulade 82
Mocha torte 99
Praline gâteau 93
Redcurrant ice cream gâteau 94
Rum and raisin gâteau 99
Spicy pear surprise 84
Strawberry gâteau 30
Tipsy ring 84
Tropical gâteau 88
Walnut and banana galette 92
Ginger:
Apple and ginger rings 49
Fruity gingerbread 27
Ginger cake 26
Ginger drops 53
Ginger ice cream gâteau 95
Gingerbread ring cake 27
Traditional parkin 27
Glacé icing 114
Granny cake 80
Guinness cake 37

Harvest fruit cake 37
Hazelnut coffee cake 22
Hazelnut cream bombe 82
Honey cake 28
Honey hazelnut gâteau 86
Honey squares 56
Humpty dumpty 100

Iced fancies 64
Icing:
    American frosting 115
    Butter icing and variations 112
    Fondant icing 115
    Fudge icing and variations 114
    Glacé icing and variations 114
    Royal icing 117
Icing equipment 18
Individual birthday cake 81

Ladybird cakes 108
Lemon:
    Butterscotch and lemon loaf 38
    Coconut and lemon cake 26
    Fluted lemon caraway cake 24
    Lemon butter icing 112
    Lemon curd cake 24
    Lemon fudge icing 114
    Lemon glacé icing 114
    Lemon honey buns 56
    Lemon maids 48
    Lemon meringues 55
    Minted lemon gâteau 86
Lime (fresh) gâteau 93
Lime glacé icing 114
Lining cake tins 15
Log cabin 107
Loganberry gâteau 90

Macaroons 63
Madeira cakes 26
Malted teabread 43
Meringues 55
Merry maypole cake 110
Minted chocolate marble loaf 45
Minted lemon gâteau 86
Minty chocolate cups 48
Mocha butter icing 112
Mocha roulade 82
Mocha rounds 52
Mocha torte 99
Mother's Day cake 76
Moulded flowers 123

Novelty cakes:
    Alphabet stacks 111
    Boat cake 103
    Book cake 106
    Bus cake 102
    Chocolate chuffa cake 103
    Chocolate clock cake 110
    Chocolate hedgehogs 108
    Cuthbert car 102

Humpty dumpty 100
Ladybird cakes 108
Log cabin 107
Merry maypole cake 110
Numeral cake 111
Treasure chest 106
Windmill cake 104
Numeral cake 111
Nutty angelica fancies 49
Nutty buns 46
Nutty fruit round 58

Oatcakes 62
Orange:
    Almond and orange puffs 54
    Apricot and orange teabread 43
    Orange butter icing 112
    Orange fudge icing 114
    Orange glacé icing 114
    Orange meringues 55

Parcel cakes 74
Parkin 27
Peach meringue, creamy 88
Peanut bars, spiced 58
Peanut cookies 62
Pear:
    Coffee and pear cake 23
    Spicy pear surprise 84
Pineapple, date and, loaf 44
Pink christening cake 69
Piping bags 18; to make 118
Piping royal icing designs 118-19, 123
Praline gâteau 93

Raisin and bran teabread 40
Redcurrant ice cream gâteau 94
Roses, piped 123
Royal icing 117; piping designs in 118-
    19
Rum and raisin gâteau 99
Runouts 122

Sesame flapjack 53
Silver wedding cake 69
Simnel cake 77
Ski cake 70
Small cakes and biscuits:
    Almond clusters 63
    Almond macaroons 63
    Almond and orange puffs 54
    Almond tuiles 50
    Alphabet stack 111
    Apple and ginger rings 49
    Banana date fingers 60
    Biscuit cups 50
    Brandy snaps 50
    Brownies 59
    Chocolate cup cakes 46
    Chocolate hedgehogs 108
    Chocolate marble squares 57
    Chocolate shortbread hearts 55

Cinnamon rings 61
Coconut crisps 59
Coconut fudge slices 52
Coffee butterflies 64
Crunchy coffee cakes 57
Fairy cakes 46
Florentines 50
Fruity bran fingers 60
Fruity oatcakes 62
Ginger drops 53
Honey squares 56
Iced fancies 64
Ladybird cakes 108
Lemon honey buns 56
Lemon maids 48
Little fruit cakes 46
Meringues 55
Minty chocolate cups 48
Mocha rounds 52
Nutty angelica fancies 49
Nutty buns 46
Nutty fruit round 58
Parcel cakes 74
Peanut cookies 62
Sesame flapjack 53
Spiced peanut buns 58
Traditional oatcakes 62
Walnut coffee trumpets 61
Snow-peaked cake 71
Spiced coffee teabread 45
Spiced peanut bars 58
Spicy pear surprise 84
St Clement's ring cake 38
Strawberry gâteau 30
Swiss roll 30

Teabread:
    Apricot and orange teabread 43
    Aromatic teabread 40
    Brazilian teabread 41
    Farmhouse loaf 33
    Malted teabread 43
    Raisin and bran teabread 40
    Spiced coffee teabread 45
Testing cakes 17
Three-tier wedding cake 66
Tipsy ring 84
Treacle, to weight 27
Treasure chest 106
Tropical gâteau 88

Valentine's cake 76
Victoria sandwich 20

Walnut and banana galette 92
Walnut cake 23
Walnut coffee cake 22
Walnut coffee trumpets 61
Wedding cakes, single-tier 68; three-tier
    66
Windmill cake 104

Yogurt cake 28